MESSAGES FROM THE COSMOS

Personal and Planetary Healing with Starbrary Quartz

To Georgie

May you be inspired and aspiring!

By Lauren D'Silva

ISBN 978-0-244-86343-2

Disclaimer: Although the author believes in the efficacy of crystal healing this book is not intended as a substitute for medical attention. You should consult a qualified physician if you have any concerns about your health.

If you are currently undergoing medical treatment, if you have mental health issues, or if you have any other issues that compromise your health, you should seek medical advice before using any of the exercises in this book.

The author will not accept any responsibility for your health and well-being when using the exercises or information contained in this book.

Acknowledgments

This book would not have happened without input from many helpers. An especial thank you to members of the Starbrary Quartz Custodians Facebook group whose encouragement has helped make this book a reality.

I invited the Facebook group members to contribute their Starbrary experiences. Many of these are included in the book. Some are profound, some serious, some joyful. Many are all three. You can be spiritual and have fun too!

I haven't rewritten their contributions, only corrected the typos. These are personal stories and so deserve to be told in the voice of the individuals who experienced them.

Grateful thanks to my husband Steve Deeks-D'Silva for his support, to my students and the participants on our Retreats and Masterclasses for their willingness to try new things.

Thanks to my son Jacob Lathbury for his photographic skills and to Charlotte Grace Hunt of The Happy Hunt for being the 'body' for the grids and layouts.

Finally gratitude to the many Star beings who have assisted us in connecting with the Starbraries and in hearing the messages they contain.

4

Contents

CW01502335

Preface

I've worked with crystals for over 20 years, both as a Crystal Therapist and as Principal of Touchstones School of Crystal Therapy. I love crystals, but I have been sceptical about the New Age hype and trendy names given to some more recent finds. When I heard the name 'Starbrary' I suspected a clever marketing ploy.

'Starbrary' was coined to describe these special quartz crystals by combining the words 'star' and 'library'. Once I connected with these crystals I realised this is an apt name which accurately reflects their nature. In my experience the Starbraries are encoded with information from the Cosmos. Unlike a traditional library these crystals also have the capacity to connect you with the source of their information and facilitate communication with that source.

Working with Starbrary quartz may lead you on a fascinating voyage of discovery into the Cosmos. I hope you will enjoy reading about the wisdom that has come through the Starbraries and that you'll also experience Starbrary quartz energies for yourself.

At the time of writing we have just entered a new decade. I sense that we must change our collective treatment of our Planet as a priority. This is our last opportunity to shift our perspective and become responsible custodians of the Earth.

I hope you will join me in sending Cosmic healing to the Earth and spreading the key Starbrary messages of love, peace, healing and unity consciousness across the Planet.

Lauren D'Silva

February 2020

Chapter One

Personal Experiences of Cosmic Energies and Starbrary Quartz

The cosmos is within us. We are made of star-stuff.
We are a way for the universe to know itself.

Carl Sagan

Personal Experiences of Cosmic Energies

I've always loved to look at the stars. As a small child I spent a long time gazing at a map of the constellations in my Mother's huge Reader's Digest Atlas. That double page spread, plus the one on Crystals of the World, kept me entertained for hours at a time.

As a young teenager I came across a book called 'The Welsh Triangle' which documented numerous UFO and ET sightings around the Fishguard area. That book made a long-lasting impression on me, but it was just one interest amongst many and I was in no way a UFO fanatic growing up. That said, I don't remember ever doubting that intelligent life exists elsewhere in our vast Universe. To deny the existence of intelligence in the Universe which surpasses our own has always seemed the height of human egocentricity to me!

When we moved to Wales my daughter saw a UFO hovering over the town just in front of our house in the middle of the night. It was 'cloaked' and would have been invisible, but for the orange sodium streetlight which was reflecting off the underside of the spaceship. She described it as a classic flying saucer shape. She was too scared to move and was worried that they might abduct me if she came to wake me up! My daughter isn't the sort to make this up and was clearly shaken by the experience.

I have had some personal encounters with Extra-terrestrial energies since I have been on the spiritual path. After splitting from my first husband a psychic told me she could sense that part of my being was Pleiadean and that it wished to reconnect with me.

Following the reading it felt appropriate to invite the Pleiadean part of my soul back. On her return I experienced a phase of intense well-being, both physically and emotionally. My spine felt straighter and stronger and I felt very peaceful and calm.

When I started dating Steve he decided to take my Crystal Therapy course. In one memorable lesson on past lives we sat opposite each other gazing into each other's eyes. This exercise sometimes reveals a glimpse of a past life self. We jolted back in surprise in the same instance and announced, "Planet of the Apes!"

We had simultaneously seen the 'intelligent ape' features on each other. Is there a real Planet of the Apes? Based on that experience I think there probably is! Is it Earth? I doubt that, but perhaps this was a glimpse of an alternate reality.

Steve has also been perceived several times as a lion-headed being. His mane of long hair probably helps, but I have seen this other being overlaying his features and several of my students have independently mentioned this. It wasn't until I passed a Glastonbury bookshop window that I associated his appearance with another planetary existence. I saw a book with distinctive lion-headed beings on the cover: The Paschats and the Crystal People by Murry Hope. Was Steve a Paschat in another lifetime?

The images on the cover of Murry's book are reminiscent of statues of Sekhmet, which makes me wonder if Sekhmet was really a being from another planet. I have long sensed a resonance with her energy. Once, when visiting her statue in the British Museum, I took her photo. Only when I got home did I realise that light seems to be shining from her mouth.

Were some of the Egyptian Pantheon of Gods and Goddesses really beings from other planets? Perhaps they brought their advanced knowledge to the Planet in ancient times and were worshipped as Gods and Goddesses.

As our relationship unfolded Steve and I began to uncover a significant past life relationship in Ancient Egypt and heal old wounds. I tell our story in 'Light behind the Angels.'

Thinking back over our experiences I was reminded of a book I read on holiday by Solara called 11:11. I'd made notes on a pad as the content overlapped with our own experiences at that time. This information didn't make it into 'Light behind the Angels' because the notepad lay buried in a drawer and wasn't uncovered until a few years after publication. Here's what I noted; bearing in mind these are my jottings and may not be an exact transcript of Solara's words. It caught my interest because our Egyptian names had started with 'An'.

The family of AN are those of us who are choosing to move into the Template of Oneness...

...denote the step down from the Starry Oneself to embodiment as humans on Earth. The AN lineage stepped down through immersion in the Celestial Realms. Here are found the Angels...

...Both the lineages of AN and ON emanate from the energy source centred in the zone of Overlap in the belt of Orion. They belong to the Council of the Elohim.

Our work to heal our past life traumas was often intense, but most of the time we could clear the energy for ourselves. Sometimes we would get stuck and ask for help, which was always available at the right time. One exceptional healer told me, "Connect to the highest vibration. You are only reaching a certain level with Archangels and Ascended Masters. You are dealing with Outer Space stuff, right out there." She told Steve that we were working 'directly with star energies'.

Janosh in the ro... th an accompan... card has its own... on etc. s explain us what) us and our

able as postcards

Arcturians" inclu... n cards with silver ...

with instructions Code net closing mechan... ns.com

)0

At the time we didn't know what to make of her pronouncements, but the very next morning I sat up in bed and announced to Steve, "It's the Arcturians!" Their name came out of nowhere, I don't remember hearing about the Arcturians before. I went downstairs to tidy the lounge for my students' arrival and picked up a little piece of paper from the floor. It was a crystal picture I'd cut from a magazine. I turned it over and there on the back of the scrap was the word **Arcturians** written in bold type. That was confirmation enough for us!

13

I was aware that the Arcturians were there for both of us and sometimes I could sense them in one of my healings, particularly where a client was dealing with 'off-planet' disruptive energies. We are by no means experts on the Arcturians, however we sense that their incredible strength comes through their unity as a race. They are a true example of, 'All for one and one for all,' which means they can call upon each other's energies for additional support whenever they need to. Can you imagine what humans might achieve with that level of co-operation?

My own sighting of UFOs came in the Spring of 2017, just a few months before we met the Starbraries. We were on holiday in rural Portugal. One night I decided to go to bed early as I was tired. Steve was watching the film Independence Day on satellite tv.

I lay down and started to read, then I heard fireworks in the distance. I decided to get up and take a look. Sure enough there was a firework display a few kilometres away in the little village of Campia. Then I looked up into the sky. I saw a stream of 'stars' across the sky above me, like a focussed beam, hundreds of them moving in formation, far too many for me to count. They were all twinkling, like lights blinking on and off. The size of each of the individual points of light was similar to that of satellites. It wasn't possible to say how high up they were, but my impression was they were out in space beyond Earth's atmosphere.

I called to Steve to come outside. He looked up. He suspected it was a plane towing a magical sparkling banner. Rather unlikely given the remote countryside we were in! He listened for the sound of an engine. Nothing, complete quiet apart from the croaking of frogs in the pond. He thought it could be something to do with the firework display, but that was all over now and the lights were still there, silently moving across the sky, far too high up to be a projection.

I am convinced there was nothing Earthly about this sight; these were spacecraft flying in formation. I tried to capture the image on video, but the specks of light were much too distant for the camera I had with me. I did capture Steve laughing and saying, "Don't get probed!" He went back to his film.

I stayed watching the skies. I noticed the 'stars' in the lead were spreading out creating a crescent-shaped formation and the ones at the back of the stream were forming more of a tail and were getting more spread out. I tried to draw it, but not being much of an artist I couldn't really capture what was happening.

The lights weren't diminishing at all, not falling or winking out like a meteor shower would, they were steadily crossing the night sky. I watched until the last lights of the 'tail' moved out of sight. I probably watched them for almost an hour. The whole thing felt like a very special treat and a real privilege to observe. I'm so grateful for the village firework display. Without their celebration to draw me outside I would have missed it all.

Almost like satellites in size but so many + all blinking - no sound at all. The first glance so tightly packed they thinfer they were, any toward, was looking for a plane - but there was none.

formed a crescent shape as they moved

My notes from the night . I apologise for the scrawly handwriting!

16

Meeting the Starbraries

My first meeting with Starbrary quartz occurred in the seemingly chance way that most significant events happen.

Steve and I were visiting our local Rock and Gem Show at the Royal Welsh Showground in Mid Wales in the Summer of 2017. In previous years we had exhibited crystals at the show, however my diary was busy so we decided that we'd just pop along as visitors and see if there was anything interesting. I had in mind that I really wanted quartz. I had found it difficult to source good quality clear quartz for my Crystal Therapy students to work with.

I made a beeline for one of my 'go to guys'. I've had some exceptional crystals from this trader in the past. There was just one large quartz point on his stall. As I stood looking at it another customer stretched her arm in front of me and snatched it up, saying, "I'll have that!" Okay, that one clearly was not for me!

I asked the stallholder if he had any other quartz tucked away under the stall. It is always worth asking as a lot of the traders bring more stock than will fit on their tables. This time I was out of luck, however the stallholder pointed me to another seller, saying he had some interesting quartz.

Gratefully we moved across the aisle and asked about the quartz. The seller said, "I've got these Starbraries from Minas Girais in Brazil." I'd never heard of Starbraries before and I immediately put it down to a New Age gimmick. There can be a lot of 'fluff and nonsense' in the naming of crystals. However, when I looked at these crystals they were the most unusual looking clear quartz I'd ever seen.

Steve and I promptly sat down on the floor beside the stall and started to sift through hundreds of clear quartz points, getting more and more excited about them as we went on. The crystals were often deeply etched and many of them were water clear in quality. I've got some etched quartz in my own collection, but these were so heavily marked, they were quite extraordinary!

We became utterly engrossed and several of my Crystal Therapy students dropped by to have a chat, amused to see us sitting on the floor. An hour or so later we'd filled a box with our favourite Starbraries and got them weighed. My crystal buying budget was completely blown. I looked pleadingly to Steve who pulled his emergency reserve cash out of his wallet, on one condition, that a striking crystal laser quartz sourced from the same area of Brazil joined our haul.

We drove home with our box of Starbraries. I felt so excited! As soon as we got back I started to unpack and wash these lovely new crystals. By now it was the end of the day and I knew that the stallholders would be packing up. I was seized with a sudden urge to raid my bank account and drive back to the Show to buy more of these unusual crystals. I controlled myself; I had already spent my entire budget on them and Steve's cash too. I carried on cleansing the crystals we had bought.

I can't remember much more about that evening apart from feeling like I was floating. Steve complained that I was completely ungrounded. I must explain that normally I am a grounded person. 'Floaty' isn't generally a word people use to describe me. I have been handling crystals for decades and I can stay well-grounded whilst I work with high vibrational crystals such as phenacite or moldavite. Why were the

Starbraries affecting me so strongly? I was intrigued to find out.

Next day I decided to explore one of the Starbraries which had particularly caught my attention with its unusual geometry. Looking from the point of the quartz down its body it has a diamond shape, highly unusual for quartz.

I sat down with the crystal to meditate and noticed there seemed to be a portal, or doorway, inside the crystal. As I focussed my mind on the portal I was transported in an instant to another world where the sky was a distinctive shade of pinky-purple. I could see some crystalline domed buildings in the distance and standing close to me were a group of slim, tall beings, all with long blonde hair and long white robes. Their appearance was androgynous; although I felt they were male and female they looked more alike than they were different. They were also silent, but I sensed they were communicating with me telepathically. I felt I was made welcome and their energy was very peaceful. I received the name 'Andromeda'.

Now I'd had a personal experience of Starbrary energy I was impressed! I was also kicking myself for not going straight back to the Show and buying the rest of these special crystals!

At the time I thought this was the first encounter I'd had with the Andromedans, however I went through some of my old journals at a later date and found a message from Moldavite which I had channelled years before, but forgotten all about:

I am the Spirit of Moldavite. When I shattered on impact with Planet Earth my consciousness was split into thousands of pieces, yet each contains a link to the whole of me.

My fall from the Heavens was no accident; it was a gift to the Earth and I do not mourn the shattering of my Self. I mirror the experience of all Creation as you went through the Big Bang and in the creative explosion your vessels were shattered and yet you too are complete unto your Selves. The separation from the whole is an illusion and it is time for a return to Unity Consciousness.

Meditate with me to connect to the wider Heavens. You look up and see the stars and they seem so far away and yet they are close. Time and space is an illusion. You can connect as easily to starlight as to the sand upon the seashore and there are as many stars as grains of sand.

You are the stuff that stars are made of and many of you are remembering other lives in other worlds. None is superior or inferior, they are all aspects of the Whole. Some races however have lost sight of their Unity, whereas others are aware of this.

I link you to Andromeda, whose civilisation is far older than any you have on Earth. You are but children in this Universe and it is now time for you to mature and take responsibility for your creations on your Planet. When you hold me you hold a piece of an older world, a place of more subtle vibration.

I wanted to find out whether my own impression of Starbrary energy was something other people might share. I decided to offer some free taster sessions with my students in the spirit of research.

I train my students to connect with their crystals in a variety of ways using intuition, visualisation and Shamanic journeying. I chose journeying to explore the Starbraries as I didn't want to influence their impressions of the crystals by leading them on a guided visualisation. By using Shamanic journeying they would gather their own insights. Afterwards I gave them questions on a feedback sheet to gather their findings.

Here are some of their initial impressions:

Can you describe the place you were taken to?
A place of white light, city with spires, huge library, floor to ceiling (books). Ocular hole in ceiling with rainbow light coming through.
Did you receive any guidance for working with the Starbrary Quartz or for the role they are to play?
Connecting to ancient power / knowledge that has been lost. Bringing through light energy.
Any other thoughts?
For me there was a 'recognition' when I first connected to the crystal energy. I feel that these crystals may also help to connect you to knowledge / skills that you have held in previous lives but forgotten. **Sharon**

Can you describe the place you were taken to?
A pebble beach with a door at the end – like a portal filled with bright white light. I was invited to take a step into the light to be cleansed. Then I was in a place suffused with purple light. There was a shaft of energetic white light beneath. The most striking image was of a column of intertwining light spiralling upwards. I think it was a caduceus.
Did you receive any guidance for working with the Starbrary Quartz or for the role they are to play?
The crystal very clearly and loudly said, "I am the cleanser, the purifier, removal of toxins." **Laura**

Can you describe the place you were taken to?

Spirit of the crystal guided me up a shaft of white light then into a whirlpool of spiralling energy which I had to allow myself to fall into. Then I came out into the centre of the crystal which was a hollow tube-like place full of spiral staircases in all directions.

The Sprit of the crystal was guiding me. It was an energy being without physical form, like flowing smoke or vapour, white but translucent, like white light separating into rainbow colours.

Did you receive any guidance for working with the Starbrary Quartz or for the role they are to play?

Was told all the stairways were paths to follow which would lead to places where guidance, information, knowledge, would be found. Zipporah

Can you describe the place you were taken to?

It was all white light full of crystals twinkling like stars all around. Meirwen

Can you describe the place you were taken to?

Started in Mediterranean, through a sand vortex and out into a white landscape / clouds.

Please describe any other aspects of your journey you felt were important:

Lightness, freshness, water, cleansing energy. Gislaine

White light was the most common experience, with several students being shown that this could be split into the colour rays, the pure colours we see when white light is refracted through a prism, most often seen in Nature as a rainbow. There was also a sense of a strong cleansing energy that could be accessed through the Starbraries. Since those early

22

days I have included an invitation to cleanse and clear our chakras into most of my visualisations with them.

There was a sense that these crystals can help us to access lost knowledge and power. This has been a theme running through our work with Starbrary quartz. I believe that these crystals are keys to ancient wisdom which has been safely locked away until this time in our evolution when we are spiritually mature enough to access it again.

Steve was told more about the Arcturians when channelling information using his Starbrary laser quartz. This crystal doesn't want to be photographed, but it has many tiny terminations forming the narrow laser point. The Starbrary laser crystal feels like it links into wisdom from across star systems. Here is what it told Steve about the Arcturians:

The Arcturians are a planet of healers. They suffer not disease. They are of peace and love. They are the helper systems. Compared to your system they are mighty in the way of universal love for that is their creed.

If you invite Arcturians from your heart to be with you, they will answer. Do not abuse their love. They can help you. You must trust in their skills and accept their love. It is a different love to that which you have experienced. It is unconditional.

Having worked with Arcturian energy I can confirm that they are exceptional healers and can assist those of us who do healing. Their energy is very strong. I remember doing a healing on Steve and inviting his Arcturian helper to work through me. I physically shook with the amount of energy being channelled through my system. Steve commented that his helper had dialled the strength down to a tiny fraction of the potential energy he had to offer so that I could handle it.

As you work with the Starbraries you may find that you make your own healing contacts with Star beings. Benevolent beings will not force their energy upon you; you can choose whether you want to work with them or not. Be respectful and if you find their energy too intense ask for it to be dialled down to a level you can use safely.

Steve's laser Starbrary told me to communicate about the Starbraries, hence this book:

It is for the One to spread the word with all that is available to her. You will help the One to translate to the correct language. We need to be heard.

Steve's Starbrary asked to speak directly to me. Here is the channelling I did with this extraordinary crystal:

Starbrary: You can work with me more easily than the Keeper (Steve) for you are accustomed to crystalline energies. They are comfortable for you and a great comfort. They form the backbone of your work. You are not confined to the Crystal Kingdom, but they are your support team and will enable you to remain strong in the coming days. We love you and respect your work.

I am a key to the other Starbrary energies. We are pleased you are communicating and connecting in your group and wish you to continue and expand this. It is a harmonious grouping and because you lead the way all present can connect to the level they are capable of.

Do source my brother and sister crystals as more need to work with you. At this time you can assist only through connecting human consciousness with the heart. Always connect through the heart; we are pleased to see you have been doing this. It is a key teaching.

Sourcing more Starbraries has been tricky as they are such rare crystals. We bought all the Starbraries the seller had left in stock and I asked him to get more when he went to the big overseas trade shows if he could. The first time he came back empty handed as the price had risen steeply, however I persuaded him to bring some from the next show which he did.

I was hoping for another shipment of Starbraries just before publishing this book, but there were none available, which was a bit of a concern as you can imagine! At time of writing I have a limited number of Starbraries in stock and I hope and trust I will be able to source more in the future.

I followed up the free taster sessions with a whole day exploring Starbrary quartz with my students. A key finding to emerge from the Starbrary Quartz Explorers Day is that the energy from the Starbrary crystals is amplified when working in a group.

One of my students suggested setting up a Facebook Group, just for the Starbraries. I went ahead and formed 'Starbrary Quartz Custodians' as a closed group. Our group has grown to become a supportive environment for us to share our insights and experiences without fear of ridicule.

If you'd like to join the Group you are welcome. I'll ask for a photo of your Starbrary quartz as your 'passport', or take a selfie of yourself holding this book and I will admit you.

Many of the exercises and visualisations in Part Two of this book were initially created for the Starbrary Live sessions I run in the group. You can read more experiences with members' own Starbraries too.

I experience some strong physical reactions when I lead the group visualisations with the Starbraries. It looks a bit strange when you view the video footage, but I have experienced shaking whilst channelling energies before and I've seen other ET channels shake in a similar way. I believe the shakes are the result of channelling a higher vibrational energy than the human energy system is used to.

Although the shakes look peculiar they are not uncomfortable. As I begin the visualisations I often experience a rhythmic side to side shaking that starts subtly and builds into a visible rocking motion. When the Starbrary energy reaches my base chakra I have a kundalini release and there is a feeling of bliss and connectedness. At that point I have to remember that I am leading a visualisation for the group as it would be easy to allow myself to float in that expanded state!

Another type of shaking developed which comes through my arms and hands, particularly when I am holding a Starbrary quartz at my heart chakra and channelling the energy for healing. It is a rapid forward and back motion which can be quite strong, ebbing away when I am coming to the end of the channelling. Again this doesn't hurt me in any way.

The Starbraries made their big debut at the Crystal Enlightenment Retreat held near Glastonbury in October 2017. I led the participants in a Starbrary visualisation. I loaned a Starbrary crystal to everyone attending, expecting that a few might want to buy theirs. In the event almost everyone experienced an instant bond with their crystal and bought it. This event confirmed the insight that the size of the group working with Starbrary energies can amplify the experience for everyone.

One of my Crystal Therapy students, Mandy, attended the Retreat and recorded an interview after the experience. She had already been experiencing off-planet energies so that aspect wasn't new to her, but the Starbrary energy was a revelation:

The first time I journeyed with it I was taken out into the Cosmos. I saw Light beings, they took me out. We hovered over their planet. It had no form, it was just golden light. They gave me a message. It was about Oneness, it was about harmony, it was about how we are all connected. They said we are connected with a golden thread, a golden ray of life that connects all of us.

Mandy went on to work with the Starbraries more intensively and wrote her Crystal Therapy Diploma thesis on them. She confirmed that the Starbraries need us to tell their story and raise awareness about the messages they contain.

Starbraries taking part in a larger group ritual for Healing the Earth at the Crystal Enlightenment Retreat 2017

Chapter Two

The Starbrary Mission

...more advanced worlds than our own are trying to communicate with us; ... a whole category of noble and beneficial mental behaviour, which appears in our societies as good conscience, humane deeds, artistic inspiration, scientific genius, is really dictated by half-understood telepathic messages from other worlds.

John Fowles, The Magus

Thoughts on Time and Space

I believe that at a time in our far history the Starbrary quartz crystals were encoded with information by a group of highly evolved Star beings. They were representatives of benevolent races who support the evolution of humanity. The Starbraries were destined to be unearthed and worked with at this precise time in Earth's transition into the New Age.

How did the Star Beings know we'd need their help now? Why did they make their preparations so long ago?

A shared belief in the passage of time is convenient for life on Earth. If we couldn't measure time then keeping our appointments, turning up reliably for work, catching a train and so on would become fraught with difficulty. Although it is practical to know what time it is, time isn't nearly as fixed as we like to believe. Over a hundred years ago Albert Einstein said,

'The distinction between the past, present and future is only a stubbornly persistent illusion.'

Physicists have proven Einstein's Theory of Relativity using atomic clocks. Time has been measured as running more slowly at lower altitudes than at higher ones. The difference in the speed of time passing is tiny whilst you are within Earth's atmosphere, but once you leave the Planet's gravitational field and travel into space it is theorised you might age more slowly than had you stayed on Earth.

We have all had personal experiences where time seems to speed up or slow down. These are so common they do not seem all that remarkable, however our state of mind clearly influences our perception of time passing. Do you remember sitting in school as a child watching the clock on the wall as the last few minutes to the end of the lesson took an eternity to pass? Or can you recall being so engrossed in a good book or a film that hours passed without you realising?

Artists, musicians and writers often lose track of time as they immerse themselves in their creative work. The name that has been coined for this is 'flow'. Experienced meditators may also take their consciousness to a state where they are not aware of the passage of time.

I believe that between our physical incarnations, when we are in Spirit, we all experience a state of timelessness. I don't think you do much clock watching when you are disembodied!

Sceptics claim that we couldn't possibly have contact with intelligent beings from other worlds because it would take 'too long' to travel from the nearest star systems to the Earth. Their reasoning doesn't allow for the possibility of accessing a higher dimension where time and space pose no such barrier.

On the evening I was editing this section I listened to an audiobook by Dr David Hamilton, which ostensibly had nothing to do with this subject. He was telling an anecdote about teaching disaffected teenage boys. He'd been enriching their maths curriculum with wide ranging discussions and mentioned talking to them about the Einstein-Rosen Bridge, a theoretical explanation of the way in which distant points in Space might be connected, more popularly known as wormholes.

Although I'd heard of wormholes, I didn't know they were rooted in scientific theory. It fits in perfectly with our contemplation of space travel. Interestingly I had been attempting to listen to a fiction book which refused to play, as did several other audiobooks I tried. Dr Hamilton's book was the first one I could get to work. I think I was meant to pay attention to his anecdote!

In our daily lives Steve and I have such regular experiences of moving beyond the physical limitations of time and space that it seems normal. Steve is a busy Shaman specialising in entity removal, with clients all over the World. He sits in his working area and from there he journeys on the Astral plane to work on his clients. His physical body doesn't leave the room, but more sensitive clients feel the effects of his work instantly wherever they are.

I've experienced the same phenomenon when sending distant healing. I can send healing to my client wherever they may be and it reaches them instantaneously. I believe that when we do our work we are using aspects of our beings that already exist on a higher dimension and are not limited by physical constraints.

Are we looking at a long cycle of human creation and destruction that we need to wake up from before a cataclysm sends humanity back into a primitive state of survival? I suspect the myths of Atlantis and Lemuria carry seeds of truth. We may have had access to higher levels of consciousness and more advanced technology in our distant past. The myth of Atlantis says we managed to destroy civilisation through our abuse of technology. We seem all too equipped to do so again.

Why Use Quartz?

I believe the Star beings chose quartz crystals to encode with their wisdom for good reason. The raw material for creating quartz crystals, silicon dioxide, is abundant on Earth. Silicon dioxide is a semi-conductor which has made it invaluable in modern technology, including computer chips. There has been some speculation that life on other Worlds could be silicon-based, rather than carbon-based as we are. Perhaps the Star beings have a strong affinity with the substance.

In my Crystal Therapy course I take students through the process of programming quartz crystal. Quartz is the most programmable of all crystals. It is versatile, with a universal healing quality that can be honed for a specific purpose. Quartz also provides a channel for white light which can be split into the colour rays, a characteristic of the Starbraries as we saw from the first exploration of their energies.

I show my students how to imprint a quartz crystal with a holographic picture symbolising their intention. The crystal projects the intention into the Universe. This is a potent form of manifestation and it must be used responsibly and with respect as the crystal may continue to broadcast an intention long after you have forgotten about it, continuing even after you are no longer in your earthly body. Crystals have a much longer physical lifespan than you do!

I believe the Star beings set their programmes into Starbrary quartz crystals knowing that they would be activated when they surfaced at this time. Unlike our programming, which leaves the quartz looking unchanged, the Star beings had the technology to engrave the surface of the quartz with their coding, creating the distinctive Starbrary markings.

Making the Transition into the New Age

I believe that many of us, especially healers, agreed to be present at this critical point in Earth's transition into the New Age, the Age of Aquarius. Our Planet needs the conscious engagement of hundreds of thousands of healers worldwide to help it through the tumultuous energies of this time.

I doubt you'd have picked up this book and read so far if you didn't sense a calling to serve at some level of your being. Your soul knows what you came here to do, even if your conscious self has forgotten.

Most of the people I connect with are aware that there is monumental change happening on the Planet. We are moving into a new paradigm and as with any major transition it may not be easy. Change is coming, like it or not, so work with your Starbraries and get yourself aligned with the new way of being!

As the shift occurs some extremely difficult behaviour is being exhibited by individuals and societies. The old beliefs and behaviours will not go down without a fight. This time is experienced as harsh by a lot of us. The Starbraries can help us ride out these challenges and bring us back to a sense of inner peace, no matter what craziness is going on around us.

I have faith that tyranny will not triumph in the long term. We are experiencing the 'death throws' of the old paradigm where power was used to control other people and the environment. This abuse of power and abuse of the Planet is unsustainable. Perhaps we are being shown the extremes to clearly underline how damaging the misuse of power can be.

As we move into the Age of Aquarius I believe we will learn to use power differently. We will understand that when we empower ourselves, we may empower others. We will understand our responsibilities to ourselves, to others and to the natural world. We will recognise that we are all connected and that we are part of the intricate web of life on Earth.

I believe the Starbraries can show us a better way to work together. By working with our crystals we become harbingers of the New Age. We might not make newspaper headlines, but that doesn't matter, the coming of the Age of Aquarius will probably not get reported in the mass media!

Moving into Unity Consciousness

Can you imagine all of humanity working together for a common goal? That is quite a stretch at the moment as we are such a competitive and warlike race! Even small, well-meaning groups tend to get caught up in disagreements and break down at this stage of our evolution.

Co-operation isn't something that comes naturally to many people, not because there is something wrong with us, but because we have been brought up to compete. We strive against one another for the best exam results, jobs, customers, votes and so on. Democracy, supposedly the most civilised way to run a country, is really one huge competition with winners and losers.

When we look at the news we could be forgiven for thinking that a goal of unity is an impossible dream, but there are some glimmers of hope. Religious leaders from differing faiths sometimes meet. Groups that are inclusive of all those who want to join regardless of skin colour, religion, sexuality, or social class do form.

Bear in mind that the news always has a negative bias. We are not informed of countless heart-warming events happening each day, just the very worst occurrences, the most shocking, or tragic. There is no balance. I suggest keeping your absorption of the news to a minimum. Don't feed yourself a diet of rolling news reports if you want to maintain any sense of equanimity.

Focus instead on how powerful we can be when we unite and align our intentions together. When we connect with each other using the Starbraries the energy is magnified enormously. Being located all around the UK when connecting on Facebook does not seem to diminish the power of our connection at all. The more people connecting in the group the stronger the energy gets.

Through the Starbraries we can co-operate in harmony and peace, even at times when we struggle to find that tranquillity in our personal lives. The Starbrary energy is a balm for the soul and never fails to leave me feeling uplifted and positive.

Human evolution is a work in progress. Simply connecting and feeling the energy of unity consciousness bathing our systems, if only for a short time, gives us a taste of what might be possible as we become more conscious beings and move away from our individual ego selves into a peaceful, aligned and unified group.

Heart-Centred Healing

Whilst Starbrary energy can clear and benefit all of our chakras it is noticeable that our heart chakras are strongly awakened by their energy. When I make the Starbrary connection described in Part Five my heart centre glows with warmth. I can feel it opening wide. It's a good feeling!

Most of us have had some heartache in our lives and will benefit from this beautiful healing energy. So many people have closed their hearts to protect themselves from feeling more pain, but to heal we need to open our hearts after they've been wounded and let love in. The ET beings connected with the Starbraries know the true meaning of unconditional love. There are no strings attached, no trade-offs, no power games. Open your heart to their loving energy.

I believe that drawing our attention from our minds into our hearts is part of the Starbrary mission. Our minds have become too dominant and we live in our heads increasingly with the additional input of mobile phones and computer technology. We often override the yearnings of our hearts with the reasoning of our minds and we do this to our detriment. We need to reconnect with the heart's wisdom if we are to evolve. When our hearts and minds are united we can achieve great things.

Were you Originally from Another World?

Is it possible that you have had incarnations in other parts of the Universe? How many other worlds might you have experienced?

I have met several people who resonate more clearly with other planetary lifetimes than with their Earth lives. Many of these are very sensitive souls; they remember where they came from and they find Earth harsh by comparison.

For those who feel ill at ease in their human bodies getting well-grounded, eating nourishing food and spending as much time out in Nature as possible may be keys to feeling more like they belong here. It is also helpful to realise that no-one takes an Earth incarnation by accident. Our Planet needs these sensitive, caring souls right now.

I feel that many of us had our origins elsewhere in the Universe, however we came here in Ancient times and have continued to experience Earth lives ever since. Steve and I know from our past life explorations that we agreed to take on human bodies in Ancient Egypt. Before we incarnated we were warned how hard this would be, that 'the purity would be lost'. Those warnings were not empty words. It is hard to be a high vibrational being and be physically incarnate on Earth. The human drama of duality draws you in and is not easily detached from.

The Starbraries provide us with a valuable reminder of what it is to exist in a higher vibrational state in peace and harmony. I think they are providing a wakeup call for those amongst us who are not as conscious of their starry origins and their true nature.

Planetary Healing

Those who know they did not originate on Earth must wonder why they have forgone a kinder, peaceful and more loving existence to incarnate on what can be a hostile and aggressive World.

More evolved souls may bring a depth of compassion as they see human suffering and witness Mother Earth's struggles to restore her equilibrium. Perhaps it is love for Gaia as a living organism and respect for the incredible potential carried within each human being that is the motivator.

Whether you sense you are of Earthly origin or not, you are here on Earth for this lifetime. When we work with the Starbraries our bodies provide a conduit for high vibrational cosmic energy to come down onto the Planet. Without us these refined energies would not reach the Earth and could not feed into the Earth's energy grid which needs support at this time.

It is theorised that all matter in the Universe originated in one intensely compact form (some say as small as a pea) prior to the Big Bang. At some deep level we are still connected with all that is.

Our innate connection means our actions can have far reaching consequences, aligning us with the theory that reality is holographic in nature. This is often referred to as the 'butterfly effect', which posits that a butterfly flapping its wings in Brazil can create a tornado in Texas. It sounds highly unlikely, but it is a metaphor to show that a seemingly small change can have huge consequences.

Think of the potential crisis caused by the declining bee populations. The bees failing could cause starvation and mass extinction.

Who is to say whether the fate of the Earth can be separated from the rest of the Universe? I believe the beings who encoded the Starbraries are working to achieve harmony and unity in the Universe. They understand that you cannot ignore the parts of Creation that don't measure up to the ideal; that to achieve wholeness all parts must be included.

Our own healing is just the same, we are the microcosm and the Universe is the macrocosm. The one reflects the other. We cannot be whole whilst we are rejecting or ignoring aspects of ourselves. Until we embrace ourselves with all our complexities and deem ourselves worthy of healing we will not be whole. The Starbraries can help us to heal our whole selves just as gracefully as they help us bring healing to the Planet.

Here is how the planetary healing came through for Gwyn:
Swell of silver-white energy into my heart chakra. Faceted leaves. Silver-white leaves carrying Starbrary loving healing energy. 'Sending out', an ever replenished supply, through my heart chakra. These 'leaves' releasing love and healing wherever they fall/land...a war zone (Iraq?), refugees, 'boat people', streets of New York...
Starbrary leaves raining down onto all the places and people. Countries...Africa, Australia, China, Nepal.
Now viewing the Earth from above...covered in these leaves...covered absolutely, bright silver-white. Eventually they 'melt' into Mother Earth...she receives this loving healing energy and absorbs it within.

Maturing as Universal Beings

The Starbraries help to open our awareness so that we recognise that we are part of the larger Cosmos. Our Sun is just one star in a vast Galaxy of stars. Our Galaxy is one of many such galaxies.

With the help of our Starbraries we can move beyond an Earth-centric viewpoint and mature into an understanding that the Universe does not revolve around our small Solar System. This is a progression from Galileo's historically blasphemous realisation that the Sun does not revolve around the Earth. What was outrageous to assert in the 16th Century has become the accepted truth in modern times.

Now we have access to technology such as the Hubble telescope which shows us how truly vast the Cosmos is. It is time to grow up as a species and realise that although we are an integral part of the whole, our home planet is not at the centre of the Cosmos.

I find it curious that modern documentaries about our Planet, such as 'One Strange Rock' cling to the notion that Earth may have the only intelligent life in the Universe. Our technology has only been able to explore an infinitesimal part of the Universe, an almost insignificant foray into the vastness of Space.

Allowing our conscious minds to accept that there are other intelligences in the Universe brings us to a more mature viewpoint. Eventually I trust we will take our place alongside our Star brothers and Star sisters.

Earth as a Cosmic Way Station

I have come across the notion of Earth as a way station several times in different places. It is believed that Earth has been a valuable place to break the journey for ET beings as they venture across the Universe, just as we might stop for fuel and rest at a service station.

Humans like to believe they are the most intelligent beings on the Planet, but that is questionable. I suspect that more evolved beings have had their bases on Earth since ancient times. In the far past they may have shared some of their technology and wisdom with humanity.

Many ancient cultures had a great reverence for the stars and effort was expended in aligning their most important structures to the Heavens. Were the Ancient Egyptians, amongst others, guided by beings from the Stars?

Helping to save our Planet may not be entirely altruistic; it may be pragmatic too. If life on Earth was no longer viable then the beings who use Earth's energy to support their travels would lose their infrastructure. Well documented UFO sightings from reliable witnesses have become so common that it is blinkered to say they don't happen.

When I started writing this book I purchased Moldavite: Starborn Stone of Transformation by Robert Simmons. I was interested to see how he had organised his findings as his book, based around the exploration of a single stone, is probably the most similar publication to this one. I dipped in and out of his book, not reading in order, just reading chapters at random.

Whilst I was reading Mandy's Diploma thesis on the Starbraries I noted a striking message:

"Earth is of universal importance
- It has a life force energy that sustains humans and off planet beings
- Our Sun is an energy giver and the life force is spread among the stars
- Earth is a beacon of Light for travellers"

And also:

"We are not alone
- We are connected spiritually to other off planet beings in different dimensions
- There are many peoples in the Universe
- They want to help us for our sake and their own
- They have visited Earth before and are among us now
- They have greater technology than us"

The very next day I read Kathy Warner's vision using moldavite at Bell Rock, Sedona in Simmons' book:

I feel that there have been space beings here for many, many moons, many centuries...(I see/remember different kinds of space vehicles coming to this place. They come down and the Earth opens and Light pours out and upwards to be taken into the bottom of the ships.)...it feels as if the vortex points are a place almost of refuelling for the ships. They come down and draw off the great energy that funnels up from the Earth.

Amongst other messages coming through Mandy's work was the urgency to act now, the need to take the lead as healers and the importance of telling the story of the Starbraries.

A Universal Translation Service

My attention was drawn four times over the space of two days to the potential for some of the Starbrary quartz crystals to provide a translation service, rather like Douglas Adam's 'babel fish' in the Hitchhiker's Guide to the Galaxy. Fortunately, we do not need to insert a Starbrary into our ear for the translation to work.

NB. never insert crystals into any of your orifices!

Thinking logically the messages that come through the Starbrary crystals are delivered in English. I expect if we were Spanish they would give us messages in Spanish. Clearly these crystals did not receive their programming in modern English and the Star beings don't speak English, therefore a translation is occurring. I channelled a Starbrary message that began:

I speak the language of Light and of necessity it is translated to your language, however its purest message can only be heard as Light. You are receiving, but it isn't possible to fully translate into words. Notice what you feel when you connect with us, that is closer to the truth.

The next day I had a new client who knew she was channelling Light Language, but didn't know what any of the unusual noises she was making meant. We were discussing the need for a translator so that the messages could be understood and shared with others. I remembered my Starbrary channeling and went to find a small Starbrary which could work with her as a translator.

It so happened that later in the day I came across a channelling which Steve had done a year and a half before with his Master Starbrary. Reading it again I noticed this guidance from the crystal:

I can help as the link between your Arcturian and you. You are but working with sign language. He understands you, but you not him. Allow me to translate.

I picked up Mandy's thesis as I wanted to reread her findings. I found I had responded to her comment that,

"Master Starbrary crystals which contain information from more than one off planet beings are the rarest and most powerful of all the Starbraries,"

With my thought:

'I am starting to wonder if they behave a bit like 'translators' between the Starbraries which come from other systems – worth more investigation.'

Sometimes I need to have the same message several times over before the penny really drops! It seems the Starbraries really wanted me to integrate this idea and communicate it to you!

Chapter Three

Identifying the Starbraries

Sic itur ad astra...
Thus one journeys to the Stars...
Virgil, The Aeneid

How do you Recognise a Starbrary?

Starbraries are quartz crystals which come from a specific area in the Minas Gerais region of Brazil. The exact location is a well-kept secret. It is therefore unlikely that you'll find any Starbraries mixed up in a 'normal' bag of quartz. Usually when people think they've found a Starbrary in this way it turns out to be a record keeper or etched crystal. These can still be fascinating crystals to work with, but they won't connect with the same Cosmic energies as a Starbrary quartz.

Having said that Amy, a member of the Starbrary Quartz Custodians Group, found herself a bargain:

I like all crystals but have such an affinity for clear quartz and I knew in my heart these two were a bit different! Although they are gorgeous 2.5×1inch water clear quartz clusters they were going cheaper than the rest because I don't think the seller knew what the marks were and thought they were 'flawed' somehow. Well of course I had to buy them, and after doing some research and was thrilled to find out they are elestial starbraries! The night they came home I just wanted to hold them. I couldn't get to sleep because of their vibrations- I felt wide awake! Besides the starbrary markings they have etching and self- healed terminations.

She shared her photos of these crystals and these crystals are very much Starbraries. How did they get mixed in amongst all the other quartz? We can't know the answer to that, but they certainly found an appreciative and grateful owner!

The most distinctive features of Starbrary quartz crystals are the markings on their surface. Starbraries look like they have been engraved. Please note the distinctive Starbrary markings are found on the surface of these crystals. Starbrary coding is not a pattern or veil inside the quartz as some have claimed.

Most Starbraries will have markings that look like cuneiform script. The Starbrary quartz triangles are usually set at a 45% angle like these. If you are sensitive to crystal energy, you'll also notice that Starbraries have a different feel about them. They have a more intense energy and hold a higher vibration compared to 'normal' quartz.

Starbrary markings shown magnified

Large Starbraries are highly desirable for their beauty and rarity, however don't overlook the little ones. We have found they work well; in fact Steve prefers these smaller crystals, finding their energies livelier. They can be 'chatty' little characters to work with and are much more affordable than the big ones. Small Starbraries are ideal if you want to work with one of the layouts I share later in the book.

Some Starbraries may have dots and dashes resembling Morse code. Rarely Starbraries will combine script-like markings with horizontal 'barcode' striations similar to those found on Lemurian quartz crystals, as you see here:

The geometry of Starbraries can be otherworldly in appearance compared to normal quartz crystals. The shapes are varied so it is hard to summarise them. Here are a couple of photos demonstrating some of the more unusual Starbrary shapes that you may find.

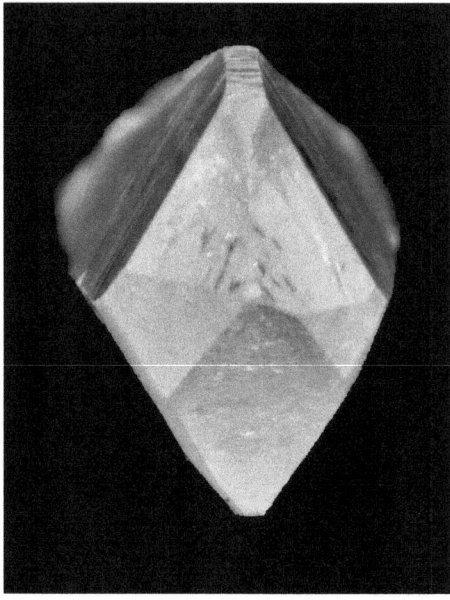

This Starbrary shape is one of my favourites to work with. It is tall and slender and gives the impression of being a 4-sided quartz crystal when viewed end on (quartz forms 6-sided crystals). This crystal is very similar to the Andromeda Starbrary quartz I connected with first.

Many of the Starbraries have additional facets which are quite unusual in quartz. These are all part of the charm of Starbaries and their quirky geometry. Here are two additional triangular facets on the side of my Isis Starbrary.

The Emergence Starbrary

This Starbrary crystal appears to erupt from within another Starbrary. It is a rare form which I have named the Emergence Starbrary. To me the central crystal symbolises the New Age rising from the old and a breakthrough into a new paradigm.

This is one of the rarest Master Starbrary shapes. This crystal enjoys connecting with the other Starbraries when I work with a group.

A small percentage of the Starbraries have a 'lightning strike' which runs down one edge of the crystal. This is not man-made damage. It appears to have resulted from a high velocity blast of energy which was used as part of the process of encoding the crystal.

The lightning strike is not something I have seen in any other varieties of quartz. The energy from Lightning Struck Starbraries is more intense and 'faster' than usual. Some of these may be Master Starbraries which can act as a 'hub' around which other Starbraries connect.

Lightning Struck Starbrary

Sherille's first encounter with her Lightning Struck Starbrary was almost overwhelming. Note that she was asked to work on herself. You may find you need to clarify your own system before you can access the potential of certain Starbraries:

I unpacked my Starbrary yesterday and it wasn't what I expected at all! I didn't get the same energy as with the other Starbraries and am sharing my immediate impression of it, I think these are more revealing as there is no time for logic to set in.

Not a lot happened until I touched the lightning strike with my thumb, then sensory overload! I was hit in the solar plexus by an energy bolt then my crown exploded with my third eye, instant connection with All That Is, rather like opening a zip. The strike isn't encoded as the others are, it's so much more. I heard it is a master crystal, as though the other Starbraries are laptops and this crystal is the NASA super-computer, the programming being done in a totally different way. There are more of them rather like the Mayan crystal skulls. They all need to be activated.

I need to raise my vibration to work with it although I feel a need to sit with it and have my other Starbraries set around me. With regards to the encoding, I think it is in the strike, layer upon layer and there is a rainbow in the centre of it that I saw when I held it up to my light. I felt it had been encoded after the other Starbraries were finished.

In addition to the forms described in this chapter, which are as far as I am aware unique to Starbrary quartz, I have found Starbraries displaying 'Master Quartz' characteristics. These include the Isis, Channellers and Transmitters, Tantric Twins and Manifestation Quartz. I have pictured those I worked with for the book with the relevant exercise.

Chapter Four

Preparing to Work with Starbrary Quartz Crystals

Keep your eyes on the stars
and your feet on the ground.
                          Theodore Roosevelt

Please read this section carefully **BEFORE** you try any of the Starbrary visualisations or layouts!

Preparing your Starbraries

Cleansing

I cleanse all my crystals before I work with them and the Starbraries are no exception. All the Starbraries that come to me are washed when I first receive them. I then cleanse them again when I have worked with them.

Do Starbraries really need cleansing? Thus far I have not come across a Starbrary quartz that feels 'sticky' or 'heavy' even after it has been hard at work.

My feeling is that cleansing all my crystals is a way of caring for them and politely thanking them for working with me. I still do this even if the crystal doesn't feel 'dirty'.

Charging

Most crystals will enjoy a sunbathe or moonbathe and will feel more 'energised' when you pick them up again. You may find starbathing suits the Starbraries better. Pick a clear night when you can see the stars.

Do you really need to charge Starbraries? Not necessarily, these crystals seem more than capable of working without being charged first. Indeed when you channel star energies through them they are left feeling zingy.

Storage

I recommend keeping your Starbrary quartz crystals separately from your other quartz crystals. You really don't want to mix them up and keeping them apart will make it easier for you to find them. I keep my Starbraries in their own wooden box lined with felt.

In the early days Steve and I tried a layout combining 'normal' quartz points with Starbraries and we got the distinct impression that the Starbraries were unhappy about this. I suspect their vibration is so different from other quartz that to attempt to combine them dampens the flow of their energies.

You may choose to explore a Starbrary quartz crystal by sleeping with it under your pillow, or on your bedside table. As long as it doesn't keep you awake all night this is one way to attune to a crystal and find out more about its energies.

I keep my favourite Andromeda Starbrary on my bedside table as I like to have it close by, but I would move it away if I was having difficulty sleeping.

Preparing your Energy

Grounding

Starbraries may connect you with strong, off-planet, energies. If you are not used to this and do not have the ability to ground yourself deeply into the Earth then these energies could be de-stabilising for you. Make sure your energy is 'well-rooted' before you try any of the practical exercises contained in this book.

If you find working with Starbrary energies is affecting your equilibrium then put the Starbraries down and take a break, focussing on your grounding and your connection with Mother Earth. If you need help with grounding use grounding crystals. My favourite grounding stone for working with the Starbraries is hematite. Goethite, magnetite or lodestone would also be excellent choices.

Starbrary energy may feel stronger than other healing energies you have encountered. You may need to work with Starbraries little and often to get used to the difference. Don't rush the process, it is fine to build up your experience of Starbraries gradually.

There are several good grounding visualisations you can work with. My recommendation is to visualise roots growing down from your feet like tree roots. Because the vibration of the Starbraries is so high you need to put your roots down correspondingly deeper into the Earth to channel these energies through you safely. I recommend dropping your grounding roots all the way down to the iron core at the centre of the Earth. You can find a recording of my grounding visualisation on my Youtube channel entitled Ground and Protect.

Protecting Your Energy

I sincerely believe that the Star beings who encoded the Starbrary crystals did so because they wanted to help the Earth and Humanity at this time of evolution and transition. If you love the feel of your Starbrary quartz that is a good sign that the beings who encoded it were harmonious and positive in their intent.

It would be naïve to suggest that all beings in the Universe are benevolent, just as it would be foolish to think all humans are friendly. My advice to you is this; if you ever pick up a Starbrary quartz and don't like the feel of it put it down again! Don't work with it. It may be the crystal isn't right for you, or it may be there is something 'off' about it.

Cleanse the Starbrary before you pick it up again. If the energy still feels unpleasant I would suggest taking it out into Nature and burying it. Allow Mother Earth to take care of the energy. This advice applies to any crystal, not just the Starbraries. You can unearth it and recheck the energy in a few months, or just leave it to rest in the ground.

Ultimately you are in charge of your boundaries and you have the authority to say a firm 'NO!' if you are not okay with any experience. Mandy told us about an occasion where she felt the ET beings she'd connected with were being too intrusive and she closed the communication down. Perhaps they were just being inquisitive, however I feel Mandy was absolutely right to assert her boundaries and shut down this interaction.

Maintaining strong boundaries and sovereignty over your energies goes for all spiritual work, not just the Starbraries. If you have an encounter you are not happy with, for whatever reason, and you would like to close it down and return to Earthly realms this can be achieved as easily as Dorothy in the Wizard of Oz clicking her ruby slippers together and saying, "There's no place like home!"

Choose a simple and distinctive physical gesture as your cue to disconnect from the experience and bring you straight back into your body. This might be linking your index fingers and thumbs in a figure eight, in front of your solar plexus chakra, symbolically creating a closed circuit and shutting off your energy from any intrusions, or you can choose something else.

Your intention rules; do not put up with anything you are unhappy with.

The Diamond of Light Protection

The Diamond of Light is a beautiful way to protect your energy field and create a peaceful, safe personal space. The Diamond we are creating is a three-dimensional shape, which can spin on its axis like a gyroscope to help you maintain your balance and equilibrium. You could use another variety of bright clear quartz, such as a Herkimer Diamond, to construct a Diamond of Light, but we have found using Starbrary crystals to create this shape is very effective and helps you stay safe when connecting with the energies of the Cosmos.

Several of my Starbraries have diamond shaped facets and are particularly apt for creating the diamond protection, but you can use any Starbrary quartz which feels right to you.

I recommend you physically move your arms when drawing the Diamond, but if you have reduced mobility just stretch them as far as you are able and imagine the rest. If you are in a public place and you feel the need to construct the Diamond you can visualise it in your mind's eye without drawing undue attention to yourself.

Don't be put off by the number of steps. Constructing the diamond follows a logical sequence and once you have done this exercise a few times you won't need to refer to the instructions.

To begin sit, or stand, with your back upright. Make sure there is at least an arm's reach of space all around you.

Hold your chosen Starbrary quartz in your right hand at your heart centre point upwards.

Now raise your arm above your head. Imagine a point of starlight emerges from the tip of the crystal to shine at the top of your aura directly above your crown chakra.

When you bring your hand back to your heart centre the starry light stays in place.

Turn the crystal to point straight downwards towards your feet. Imagine a starry point of light emerging from the crystal directly below your feet at the same distance from your physical body as the one above your head. The ground is no barrier to the light.

Bring your hand back to your heart centre and notice the two points of light. Imagine a beam of brilliant white energy flows from the starry light above your head and runs straight through the centre of you to connect with the starry light below your feet.

Hold your right hand straight out to your side level with your heart centre and again watch a point of starlight emerging from the crystal.

Pass the crystal to your left hand and stretch it out to your left side and watch as a starry light emerges.

Watch as another bright beam of light flows from the starry light on your right side, straight through you to the starry point on your left side.

Now hold your arm outstretched directly in front of you on your midline, holding the crystal point outwards level with your heart centre. Imagine another starry light blossoming from the tip of the crystal.

Imagine that you can hold your crystal the same distance directly behind you in line with your spine, level with your heart centre. If you have the flexibility you can hold your hand behind your heart centre with the crystal pointing outwards. In your mind's eye you see a point of starry light emerging from the tip of the crystal and watch as it remains in place behind you.

As you watch these two points of light you see a beam connect from the starry light at the front of you, flowing through your heart centre to the starry light at your back.

You have formed a three-dimensional cross of light. Now you can create the sides of your Diamond. Visualise four straight lines of starlight which flow from the point above your head to connect with the four starry lights around you.

Now see four more beams of light connecting the point of light beneath your feet to the four starry lights around you.

You should feel like you are in a stable structure of brilliant light, You can fill in the shape with bright Light, creating 8 clearly defined sides for your Diamond if you wish. You will probably use white light, but you might sense the Diamond spontaneously filling with another brilliant colour.

You may notice your Diamond wants to rotate or spin on its axis. Let it move as it wishes to, you can even set it in motion around you if you wish. Your Diamond can act like a gyroscope to keep your energy stable no matter what is going on around you.

The more you use the Diamond of Light the easier it will be to construct. If you don't want to use the Diamond of Light use another strong protection you have faith in before you work with the visualisations and other exercises in this book.

After putting the protection in place I sensed that the diamond was following the earths axis and that some sort of axiatonal alignment was taking place. Then when connecting with the star I felt as though the energy had connected with the diamond and I had become a beacon sending messages out across the planet. Was so absorbed in what I was sensing I became oblivious to the rest of the visualisation.

Cathy

Thank you, Lauren - that was fun:) moving the starbrary around felt very ceremonial. My diamond had transparent, rainbow-iridescent sides (like angel aura quartz, but "more" because... Starbrary), and it spins anti-clockwise, but very, very fast - too fast to see.

Nicola

That was fabulous. Loved drawing the shape around the body and Starbrary light through - it really connected strongly. Once in place the top areas of the structure were a mixture of clear and cloudy whilst the bottom corner was a pale green which travelled and filled the shape up towards my stomach (which was very soothing as I had a stomach ache...not now though!). My sacred structure didn't feel the need to spin but swayed from side to side as if rocking me, very gentle and calming. A few fleeting pops of pale blue along the structural lines of the shape before I concentrated on clearing chakras. Wonderful, thank you so much.

Lisa

Shaking and Heat

You may, or may not, experience some energetic side effects when you work with the Starbraries. As I mentioned I often experience rhythmic shaking when I work with the Starbrary energies. It is most pronounced when I am leading group work and more subtle when I am working on my own. I do not find the shakes painful or uncomfortable. I believe the shakes are caused by very high vibrational energy being channelled through the body.

Unless you find the shaking unpleasant, I would advise you to relax and 'go with the flow'. If you don't like it put the Starbrary down, check your grounding, go and have a rest, or do something mundane in the physical world.

You may find you move in a different way. Nicola says:
When I'm channelling the starbrary energy, as it descends it spins, which makes my upper body move slightly also in a circular movement.

The sensation of glowing heat is commonly reported when working with Starbraries. Personally, I find this very pleasant and the warmth is often centred around my heart which feels lovely. Again, I think this is due to the large amount of energy coming in when you work with Starbraries.

My starbraries were red hot before we began, I felt so much heat and energy throughout. I kept hearing Utopia constantly. It was beautiful.

Josie

That was brilliant! I felt SO much heat, I thought I was going to combust!

Kerry

71

Keeping a Personal Development Journal

I encourage you to start a personal development journal if you don't already have one. Starbraries may give you some interesting insights and experiences. Writing these down can be valuable and means you don't have to remember everything.

I have already described how reviewing my own notes has given me some 'light bulb' moments and helped me to integrate Starbrary messages that would have been lost without my record keeping. Your experiences won't always make sense at the time but looking back you may pick up on patterns and the meanings may fall into place.

I would not have been able to write this book, or 'Light behind the Angels', without keeping my journals. I will remind you to note your experiences in your journal at the end of the exercises in this book. I find writing in a lovely notebook motivating, but you can just keep a folder of notes or voice record your findings if you prefer.

Getting to Know your Starbrary Crystal

I recommend attuning to the energies of a crystal you wish to work closely with. By deliberately tuning into the energies of a crystal you become more familiar with it. This is a way to bond with your crystal and strengthen your relationship with it. Once you have connected with a crystal in this way you may decide to keep it in your personal collection rather than allowing others to touch it as it will be imbued with your energy.

One of my students, Juliette, found she wanted to introduce herself formally to her Starbrary crystal by giving it her thumb print.

Hi Lauren, thank you so much for my Starbrary! Wow it certainly has arrived! The first thing I wanted to do was touch it to give it my DNA. The urge was to put my thumb on the main face and spiritually put my print on it. The next day I showed it to my husband and he said he could see a thumb print on it, which I had not told him about.

Another student, Carol, found herself drawn to hold her Starbrary in a specific way, similar to a yoga mudra. She then researched her Starbrary which she felt was connected with Cassiopeia:

The first thing I found when I looked up starbrary crystals and links to Cassiopeia was so fitting —'Each crystal has various ways of being held which facilitates the release of information, within each position (hand/finger?) revealing a different layer of information depending on the hold'.

Try this simple exercise when you are getting ready to work with a Starbrary for the first time. Do your grounding and protection before you begin.

Take some time to study the appearance of your Starbrary quartz. Look carefully at the markings. Notice its geometry. See how its surfaces reflect the light.

Now close your eyes and sense the Starbrary markings by brushing them with your fingertips. Imagine you could read these impressions, like someone reading braille. If you could read them what would they say?

Notice whether your Starbrary would like to be held in a certain way. Does the crystal feel more comfortable held in your left hand, your right hand, or in both hands? Is there a place where your thumb needs to rest? Which of your other fingers need to be in contact with the crystal? Be playful, trying out different hand positions until one feels just right.

Now imagine you are saying, 'Hello,' to your Starbrary. By greeting the crystal you may open up a dialogue. This communication may take the form of words, feelings, images, or other sensations such as heat. Go quiet and let your Starbrary respond in whatever way it wants to communicate with you.

When you are finished thank the Starbrary and put it down. Check your grounding, have a drink of water and then write up your impressions in your journal.

Channelling Starbrary Messages

First do your grounding and protection. Sit with a journal or notebook open in front of you. Hold your Starbrary in one hand and a pen in the other. Relax and let your mind become quiet and receptive. Write down any messages as they come to you. Don't edit them, or even read them until afterwards. You may be surprised by how talkative some of these crystals are!

When I channel with the Starbraries I close my eyes and I experience some rapid eyelid fluttering and see a lot of light coming in behind my eyelids before the words start to flow. You may experience channelling differently. It is always an option to come out of the light trance state and back to normal waking consciousness if you are not comfortable with the messages or how the experience feels.

Close down by thanking the crystal, then putting it down, checking your grounding and having a drink of water. Now you can read what has come through.

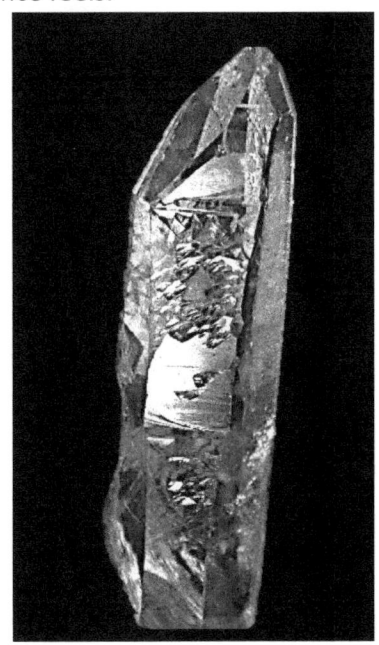

Here is my initial channelling from the pictured Starbrary:

I speak the language of Light and of necessity it is translated to your language, however its purest message can only be heard as Light. You are receiving, but it isn't possible to fully translate into words. Notice what you feel when you connect with us, that is closer to the truth.

There is a gathering of like-minded people now and you are part of that. The help that is being brought onto the Planet now is being received, but it is not always communicated, because to communicate publicly you must be seen and not many are ready to expose themselves at this time. We understand, yet to be helpful you must communicate the wisdom that is transmitted. You must group together. You must connect. Isolated individuals cannot bring change. Unite.

The Light is flooding onto your Planet, but it needs you to channel it into the Earth and to your fellow beings. We don't speak of humans, we speak of all beings. So many sentient beings whose rights are being neglected; both those in the physical and those of higher dimensional forms.

All suffer from the madness and greed that has overcome humanity as a whole. This must be reversed if any of you are to survive on Earth. It is simply not an option to continue business as usual. You must model a better way of being.

Do not be distracted. This is important work and we are relying on you to share the wisdom you receive. When you unite your energies are strong and the connection is exponentially stronger. Group together more often.

A Starbrary Crystal Cave

This is a variation upon the Crystal Cave visualisation I use with my Crystal Therapy students for attuning to a crystal. It is a way to get to know an individual Starbrary and to find out what it has to teach or show you. Some Starbraries may contain a lot of information, too much to comprehend in one visit, therefore be ready to repeat this visualisation as many times as you need to.

Follow your intuition when exploring the Starbrary Crystal Cave. Be polite and respectful to any Star beings you meet. Remember your manners as you are the visitor to the crystal. If you are uncomfortable at any point and want to end the experience simply retrace your steps.

Starbrary Crystal Cave experiences will vary widely. You may just go and relax in the Starbrary healing energy, or you may be taken on a fabulous adventure to another world.

Before you begin do your grounding and protection.

Holding your Starbrary examine it visually, taking note of the encoded surfaces, the shape, any internal features, the way it reflects the light. Notice how the crystal feels in your hand, the physical weight, the surface texture, any energetic sensations, such as tingling or warmth.

Now close your eyes and take a few deep breaths. Imagine you are standing in a warm meadow holding your Starbrary quartz. It is very peaceful here. The Sun is low on the horizon and the first few stars are just starting to show in the sky which is streaked in the West with glowing gold, orange, pink and turquoise from the sunset.

You can hear the sound of the sea. As you walk towards the setting Sun you see the ocean spread before you, the waves dappled with gold. You come to the edge of a cliff and looking down you see there are steps cut into the cliff face.

You climb down the steps carrying your Starbrary with you. When you get to the bottom you step out onto the beach.

You breathe the clean sea air and hear the relaxing sound of the waves lapping on the shore. Take a walk along the beach carrying your Starbrary until you find a place where you would like to relax and take in the beauty of the scene. You place your Starbrary quartz carefully on the beach in front of you with its point upright.

As you watch your crystal begins to grow, larger and larger. Soon it is the size of boulder, then it is as tall as you are and it continues to grow until it is towering above you, a magnificent Starbrary quartz crystal.

You walk around your crystal, marvelling at its beauty, admiring the markings which now appear like hieroglyphics on the surface. You feel a connection to this ancient crystalline language as you run your fingertips across them. It is as though you are reading the meaning through your hands. There is something deep within you which understands the encoded message.

Walking around your crystal you ask it to show you a point of access. You may find that one facet of the crystal hinges open for you like a door, or you may be shown a crevice or tunnel you can move through. You will be shown a way inside your Starbrary if you are ready for the experience.

Make your way right into the centre of your Starbrary where it opens into a vast crystal cave. Look around yourself. You may be able to see through the translucent walls of the cave. Perhaps they glow with an inner light.

What do you notice about this crystalline space? Are there stairs or corridors to explore, or is this one large space? Is there anything inside the cave? Maybe there is a healing pool, a seat, or a place to lie down.

Perhaps you are alone, or is there a Star being waiting to converse with you, or to give you healing, or show you something?

Maybe there is a glowing portal which you feel drawn to step into? If it feels right, you may step inside and find out where it takes you.

You might feel like you are having a download of information and you may not know what it means yet. The meaning may unfold as you work with your crystal.

Enjoy the energy of the Starbrary for as long as you like, allowing yourself to be bathed in its beautiful light.

When you are ready to leave thank any Star beings you met and thank the Starbrary. If you went through a portal you will find a matching portal to step back through which will return you safely to the Starbrary cave. Make your way out of the crystal by the way you came in.

You step back onto the beach and you notice that the Sun has set whilst you have been inside your crystal and now the sky is full of stars. One of them is shining brightly above you and you know that this star connects with your Starbrary.

You watch as your Starbrary begins to shrink back down in size, smaller and smaller, soon becoming the same size as you are, then continuing to shrink until it returns to its original size. You pick it back up from the beach and feel gratitude for the closer bond you have with your Starbrary now.

You walk back along the beach carrying your crystal and making your way by starlight to the steps which lead you back up the cliff. Make your way up the steps, coming all the way up, until you step back out into the meadow.

Take a few deep breaths, become aware of the floor beneath your feet and the chair you are sitting on. Bring your attention back to the here and now and have a stretch.

If you feel at all 'spacey' pick up a grounding stone such as hematite or sit with it between your feet whilst you visualise your grounding roots connecting you firmly to Mother Earth. Write up your journal.

Here are a few of the experiences members of the Starbrary Quartz Custodians Facebook group reported:

Headed beyond the Sun. In Fact travelled so close I thought that's where I was going. Saw beings with features not dissimilar to that of the Egyptian death masks glowing with a golden light. No real physical form almost like someone had drawn them with a pen of gold light. Loved the experience with my latest Starbrary. Think I was somewhere within the seven sisters. Cathy

I began the meditation guided by Lauren, left the meadow and bounded down to the beach. However, I couldn't stay on the beach but dove into the water with my Starbrary, deeper and deeper. The water was crystal clear and I didn't need to

breathe. I placed my Starbrary on the sandy bottom and watched it grow until it burst through the surface of the ocean, I swam around exploring the wonders of it and entered via a large temple door into a vast cathedral-like hall, empty, yet welcoming and felt myself grow and grow and start rising up the crystal. When I reached the ocean's surface it gave way to a wonderful, bright, glowing, silvery gold energy.

The top of the crystal opened and fell back on itself forming a lotus blossom and I was sitting in the middle of it. I was aware that in the distance, all around, were the heavens. I focused my attention back on the crystal and realised that at the end of each petal was a light being and they were channelling light into my crown, I could feel the light intensely and could feel this happening in my earthly body in my house flowing through me into the Earth and charging the grid I saw created in the first Starbrary meditation. I am to sit and connect each day if possible and this connection will become ever stronger.

I did not want to end the visit but came back into the crystal and found I was quite ethereal but regained my substance on leaving the crystal. I had placed my crystal on a sandy floor, but now it was surrounded by a stunning undersea garden! My crystal regained its original size and we swam to shore.

When I initially swam down with my crystal I felt Atlantis and then the Star Beings who founded Atlantis and helped "seed" the Starbraries. Sherille

I loved being inside the crystal, mine was full of books, shelves full of books, a library of them, and when I looked at the books a lot were on science, physics, etc. I went to this planet I think it's Alpha Centauri? Very interesting, feel my understanding of them and how we are to work together has strengthened. Josie

Beam Me Up Starbrary

This method of connecting with the 'home planet' for each Starbrary was inspired by Star Trek and the famous line, "Beam me up Scotty!" I was asking for a safe way for participants to connect with the planets their personal Starbraries resonated with. The Universe is a big place and I didn't want anyone to get lost! I was shown a tube of bright light coming straight down around the holder of the Starbrary, just like the transporter beam from Star Trek. The tube of light takes the holder directly up to the source planet. Unlike Star Trek your physical body will stay firmly on Planet Earth, however your Astral body can travel across time and space with ease.

This is an opportunity to meet Star beings from the races responsible for programming your Starbrary. You might ask for their guidance and help, both on a personal and a planetary level. So far we have identified Starbraries that connect us with Andromeda, Arcturus, the Pleiades, Sirius, Cassiopeia, Lyra and Orion. I can't predict which system your Starbrary will connect with, you will have to find out for yourself.

You could play a Shamanic drumming track to accompany your journey or you may choose a piece of music you find relaxing. Pick something which will not pull you out of the light trance state with sudden crescendos or vocals!

Choose just one Starbrary crystal for this experience so that you don't get drawn to two different locations in the Universe at the same time. That could get uncomfortable!

Before you begin do your grounding and protection.

Start by getting comfortable, sitting upright or lying down. Hold your chosen Starbrary at your heart centre pointing upwards towards your throat as you prepare to travel into the Universe.

Set a clear intention that you will be taken directly to the planet that your Starbrary connects with and that you would like to meet with the Star beings from the culture who encoded the crystal.

Now imagine a clear starry night sky above your head. One star shines more brightly than any of the others. That star is the sun closest to the planet where the Star beings who encoded your Starbrary abide.

A tube of light comes down from that planet and drops around you. Imagine turning around and seeing the light surrounding you on all sides. This is a protective light beam which will allow you to journey safely and easily across the vast distances of space.

You feel as light as air and sense yourself rising in the beam of Light and being drawn to the home planet. You may feel like you are travelling fast, almost instantly arriving at your destination, or you may rise more sedately through the stars. Allow the pace to come naturally and relax with it, you will know when you get there.

Once you arrive look around you and take in all the details. If you meet Star beings then introduce yourself. You may ask if they have any information, skills or wisdom they want to share with you. They may want to show, or tell, you something. They may also have questions for you. Spend as much time as you need communing with these beings.

When it is time to leave, thank any beings you met. Look around and commit this scene to memory. Now you sense the tube of light settling all around you again. This time the journey through the tube takes you back to Planet Earth. You sense yourself begin to travel and you may zoom down, or float down, whatever is right for you, protected and surrounded in light all the way down to the Earth and right back down into your physical body.

Have a stretch. Feel your feet firmly on the ground and be aware of fully inhabiting the physical body all the way to your fingertips and to the end of your toes. If you feel at all spacey or light-headed pick up your grounding stone and have a drink of water before you go back into normal life. Write up your journal.

Journeying to ask for assistance from the Star beings who connect with the Starbraries has resulted in some big cleansings. Clearing accumulated debris from our energy fields and raising our own vibration is of vital importance if we are going to be able to reach our potential as healers.

I received some deep healing. The beings were like emerald crystal light forms. They surrounded me and I was put in the centre of a light form crystal lotus and my heart raised up high above my body but was still attached to me by muscles/ strings. It cleansed out all the pain and remaining debris in between (it aired my heart) and then my heart attached itself back to me. It was a different heart, my heart but cleansed and much lighter, free. Then I had a similar experience but with my intestines, but on a much milder scale as that part of my body still needs some more work (I haven't personally advanced so much with that area as I have with my heart - so I still have some more work to do there before they can assist in a more profound way - everything has its time). They blasted me with healing and light. It was going through me till I became the light and was able to carry that to others. That's what it felt like I was being prepped for. I travelled a long way to see them!

Renata

I originally placed my starbrary on my heart chakra , but quite early on I noticed my throat chakra was uncomfortable so moved it there. I found myself seeing many different people, as though I was looking through a lens. Some were mythical looking creatures, dwarfs, green men, a Moses looking man. I was communicating with a source and when I began questioning all the differences I was seeing I was told that we are all mass (energy) and it is you making the form. At this point I was just completely energy with energy. My hands were tingly and I feel my starbrary is all about equality. The name I got was Andromeda, which I can't remember knowing this before the journey, so I am sticking with it.

Angela

I connected with a new starbrary I own, was taken through a wormhole, as we went to another universe or galaxy. Where I went I can't describe fully, it was just a blissful place, devoted to peace, harmony, healing. It's one of 3 such planets or bases where any of us can visit whenever we want. It was very beautiful, lots of beings including Lyrans? I met a monk in a temple, I was told of updates on my brain currently occurring with the energy shifts on earth, things coming online, can't really say, but I felt lots of healing in my head, Alta major in particular. It was incredible Lauren, thank you xx

Josie

Making a Starbrary Gem Essence

In a surprisingly literal sense all life on Earth is extra-terrestrial. This is scientific fact, not a belief. Human bodies are around 60% water, with more in certain parts of our anatomy, for example your lungs are around 83% water. Here's the astonishing thing: water did not originate on Earth! All the water you can see, all the water in your body, every drop in the oceans, arrived on our Planet from outer space. Scientists believe it was carried here by meteors and asteroids. I find that quite mind-blowing!

Water doesn't 'behave' according to the normal laws of physics. I've been aware of watery weirdness for a while as I teach gem essence making. In theory water should be a gas at room temperature, not liquid. When water freezes it floats, yet it should sink. Scientists haven't solved the puzzle of why water behaves so strangely, but maybe it is because of its extra-terrestrial origins. It is these unique properties of water that make life on Earth possible. We owe our very existence to the gift of water from the Cosmos.

Water has the capacity to hold information and it can be imprinted by whatever it is exposed to. This special quality was studied by Masuro Emoto who conducted experiments by capturing photos of water crystals. When exposed to the vibration of prayer and blessing the water crystals he photographed were very beautiful. Exposed to harsh energies and negative statements the crystals produced were disrupted and ugly. Emoto's book 'Messages in Water' contains colour plates of many of his experiments. You can also see a lot of his work on the internet.

When we expose water to our crystals the water can take on the vibrational energy of the crystal. By drinking the imprinted water we can take the crystalline energy into our system, infusing every cell of our bodies.

Gem waters are very simple to make. Ensure you are using crystals that are clean, non-toxic and won't dissolve or fragment in water. Starbrary quartz is ideal for this. Drinking a glass of Starbrary water will probably feel stimulating. Don't drink a glass just before bedtime unless you are a very sound sleeper! Gem waters don't store well, make them fresh on the day you want to use them.

Gem essence making is a bigger subject and professional training is advised if you want to make essences from a range of crystals, especially if you want to give them to other people. Making gem essences using Starbrary quartz for your personal use is reasonably straightforward, however.

If you have several Starbrary quartz crystals choose one that feels right for gem water or essence making. Note which one you chose in your journal as you may gain more insight into that Starbrary by using the water or essence.

For a Starbrary gem water you will need:

A Starbrary quartz crystal

A jug – preferably glass

Spring or filtered water.

Method: Wash the crystal so that it is energetically and hygienically clean. Place the crystal carefully in the jug and cover it with the water. Leave it for a few hours and then you can remove the crystal. Drink just one glass to check the effect isn't too strong before you drink any larger quantities.

For a Starbrary gem essence you will need:

A Starbrary quartz crystal

A small clear glass bowl (big enough for your Starbrary to lie down in the bottom)

A small glass jug

Spring water – freshly collected from a natural spring if you have access to one, but bottled spring water will work. Ideally buy it bottled in glass if you can get it.

Unbleached Coffee filter papers

Two small glass dropper bottles which have been sterilised. 10ml bottles are big enough

Labels & a pen

Brandy or Vodka as preservative – you can use vinegar instead if you are avoiding alcohol

Method: Choose a clear starlit night; you may pick a night which feels astrologically significant if you wish. You need to be able to see the starlight as it needs to shine into the bowl of water. If you live in a city with too much street lighting you might need to travel into the countryside. Wrap up warm!

Make sure your Starbrary quartz is hygienically clean by giving it a wash. Now put it in the bottom of the glass bowl and add spring water to cover. Leave it for at least a few hours, or overnight, in starlight. You will intuit how long the essence needs.

When the Starbrary Quartz water is ready filter out any bits that have floated into the bowl using a coffee filter paper held over a jug. You then pour the filtered water into a sterilised glass bottle to the halfway mark. Top up with vodka, brandy, or vinegar as a preservative and cap it.

Label the bottle with the date and Starbrary Essence 'Mother'. You can drink the remaining water that you have filtered or use it in a bath if you like.

Your Starbrary essence will go further if you make a second bottle from the original 'Mother' bottle. Allow a day or two for your bottle of Mother essence to 'settle'. Fill the second sterilised bottle half full of spring water and add drops of essence from the Mother bottle. I like seven drops for Starbraries, but you can use a different number of drops if it feels right to you. Top up the bottle with vodka, brandy or vinegar as preservative and cap it. Label the bottle as Starbrary Essence 'Stock' This is the bottle that you will use to take your drops from.

Keep your Mother essence bottle somewhere cool and dark and it should last for several years, meaning you can refill your Stock bottle using the same method whenever you need to. If you are using vinegar as your preservative the shelf life will be shorter and you may wish to refrigerate it. It should still last for some months.

Keep your essences away from strong electromagnetic fields. Don't carry them in a bag with a mobile phone or put them by your computer as they will be ruined.

You can take drops of essence in a glass of water or directly under your tongue, whichever you prefer. Be aware it is possible to get a healing crisis from taking gem essences until your body gets used to their energy. Rest if you need to. Watch out for any effect on your grounding and carry a grounding stone with you if you notice you are getting light-headed. You can also put drops into water in a mister bottle and use it as a spray for your aura – it will only last a few days if you use water as a base, but you can make refills easily.

Keep a note in your journal of any effects, including any interesting dreams you have.

You may like to use your Starbrary essence or drink a glass of Starbrary water before you sit down to do the Starbrary visualisations and layouts in this book.

I made my first Starbrary essence in Winter so the beautiful clear starry night was also a cold and frosty one. I had to allow time for the essence to thaw out next day before I could bottle it. The frost doesn't seem to have diminished the essence in any way – it feels clean and crisp.

Chapter Five

The Cosmic Connection

Our feeblest contemplations of the Cosmos stir us - there is a tingling in the spine, a catch in the voice, a faint sensation, as if a distant memory, of falling from a height. We know we are approaching the greatest of mysteries.

Carl Sagan, Cosmos

The Cosmic Connection

Over time this visualisation has become my favourite way of linking to Starbrary energies and I begin most of the online group sessions in this way. It is straightforward and has proven dependable. The Cosmic Connection helps to clear your channel and brings high vibrational energy down through your chakra system and then grounds it onto the Earth. In this way you raise your personal vibration and become a clearer conduit for these energies to become available for Planetary healing. Remember to do your grounding and protection before you begin.

Sit with your back upright, which helps you channel energy more smoothly through the Sushumna, the main energy pathway in your body, located in your spine. Hold your chosen Starbrary to your heart centre. I hold mine point upwards. If you wish to you may direct the Starbrary crystal to each of your chakra points in turn as you work.

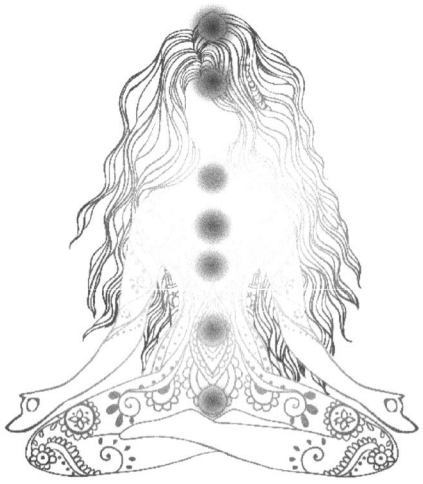

NB. All the main chakras apart from the crown and the base chakra have front and back aspects to them.

Visualise a night sky, a beautifully clear night sky embroidered with stars. The star which connects with your Starbrary is shining brightly, much brighter than any of the other stars.

You see a brilliant beam of light coming down from the star, coming straight down to you. Allow this pure beam of light to flow into your crown. There the energy cleanses your crown chakra, clearing any debris which may be getting in the way of making your Starbrary connection.

Once your crown feels clear you invite the energy to drop down to your brow chakra. You see the channel of light flowing to your third eye. You feel your third eye being cleared, front and back. It is being cleansed of any blocks which inhibit your ability to perceive, so that you may see more clearly and gain more insight.

Now see the channel of light flowing down to your throat chakra. Feel the Starbrary light clearing and cleansing your throat, front and back, helping you to speak your truth and express yourself without fear.

You see the channel of light flowing down to your heart chakra. Feel it clearing your heart chakra, front and back. The Starbrary energy helps you to centre yourself in love and peace. It helps you become more open-hearted. You may see the Starbrary quartz at your heart lighting up brilliantly and radiating with light.

Now you can see the channel of light flowing down to your solar plexus chakra. Feel the Starbrary light clearing your solar plexus, front and back. It is helping you to feel more empowered, more confident and energised. You know you can accomplish the things you came here to do.

You see the channel of light flowing down to your sacral chakra. Feel the light clearing this chakra front and back. You are a naturally creative and sensual being. Enjoy making things, enjoy making love, enjoy the pleasures of your physical body.

Now you are aware of the channel of light flowing all the way through the column of your chakras from your crown, through your spine, right down into your root chakra at the base of your spine. The light is clearing your connection to the Earth so that you feel safe and secure. When your base chakra is clear you will have an abundance of physical energy.

Once your base chakra is full to overflowing with light any excess flows down your legs and through your feet, into Mother Earth. As it does so it helps you to feel more grounded and connected to the Earth and it nourishes her energy with Starbrary light.

Know you are a vessel for the Light, a vessel for peace and for harmony.

At this point you can move onto any of the other Starbrary experiences which begin, 'Make the Cosmic Connection.' Alternatively you can end your visualisation by watching the beam of energy going back to the star and making sure you are grounded before going about your day.

As you spoke of each chakra, my Starbrary was 'drilling' down through each one (refreshing not unpleasant as it might sound!!)...clearing more old unnecessary energy patterns as it went (like the pencil shavings that come off when you sharpen it) A very refreshing yet caring and loving sensation.

Gwyn

94

For Personal Healing

The Starbraries and the Star beings who connect with them can provide exceptional healing. The best healers I know are not from this Planet and I trust the ones the off-planet healers I have worked with completely.

All you need to do is ask for healing once you have made the Cosmic Connection. Just allow the Starbrary energy to flow to the place in your body you are holding tension, discomfort, or disease.

Providing you are happy with your connection (a good connection will feel positive and heart-warming) be ready to truly let go of your issues. No healer, however powerful, can deliver you from an affliction until you are ready to release it, physically, mentally, emotionally and spiritually.

By working on ourselves with love we become a more positive force in the World. It is not selfish to use the Starbraries to heal yourself. You are as worthy of healing and love as anyone else. It is more selfish to ignore your own issues!

Those who carry unresolved anger, resentment and shame create chaos in the World. Once you truly love and accept yourself you will radiate a beautiful light which touches everyone you meet.

Make the Cosmic Connection (page 93).

Scan your body and notice whether any area is holding tension, discomfort or pain. Ask for the beautiful Starbrary light to flow to that place now. Allow it to dissolve the pain, allow it to dissolve the discomfort, allow it to dissolve any tightness.

The Star beings you connect with through the Starbraries may be truly amazing healers. Be ready to accept their healing if it is offered. Know you are worthy of healing. Allow their healing in.

As you consistently work on yourself you will be radiating out a brighter light. Your light touches others, and so you create a ripple effect that flows out to everyone around you. As you literally hold more light in your system others will notice.

Some people will be drawn closer to you and they will benefit from that light. Others may move away from you because the light scares them; it illuminates dark places in themselves that they aren't ready to look at yet. It is not your job to determine how people will react to your light; it is not your role to control their reactions.

Your role is simply to be yourself, holding your light as clearly as you can, forgiving yourself when you get things wrong, which will happen sometimes. You are human, you are a work in progress. You need to be patient and forgiving with yourself and others. Allow yourself time to change. You will change, know you are changing right now.

When you are ready say thank you to any beings who helped you with their healing energy. Say thank you to the Starbrary itself. Allow the beam of energy to go back to the star.

Become aware of your roots going deep down into Mother Earth, grounding you securely. Take a few deep breaths and bring your consciousness back into the room. Pick up a grounding stone if you need one and write up your journal.

Just want to share today's Starbrary experience. This morning I got up early to meditate and at first thought I was going to use my Lemurian seed but was then drawn to use my Starbrary. During the meditation I was guided to use it to clear all my chakras, it did a great job, clearing a lot especially from my throat chakra. It was a wonderful meditation that really set me up feeling clear for the day.

Later on this afternoon I was driving along the A55 in North Wales where there are stretches with the most amazing views and myself, and my son were marvelling at the beautiful sky. All of a sudden I was taken right back to my first ever meditation with the Starbrary where I had seen a landscape that was almost like a desert but whiter with rolling hills. The exact (and I mean completely exact) landscape was there is cloud form clear as anything. I was amazed!!!

Michelle

Towards Wholeness

I first gave this visualisation on All Hallows, the day after Halloween, which is more properly called All Hallows Eve. All Hallows is a hallowed, or holy, day. It is an auspicious day for working with the theme of wholeness as the word holy is closely connected to the word whole. To be whole is to be holy. You don't have to wait until 1st November to do this visualisation however!

As we move towards a state of Unity consciousness we need to come to an acceptance of our whole selves. You cannot reject part of yourself and be whole. Once we accept ourselves in our entirety, we can become the instigators of great change in the world around us. You can't change the outside until you change on the inside. As the saying goes, "Be the change you wish to see in the World." These words of wisdom are usually attributed to Ghandi, although some dispute this. Whoever first uttered them they carry truth.

This visualisation is a further exploration of the work we began in our visualisation for personal healing and self-acceptance. This is a strong theme coming from the Starbraries. Don't think you can heal the World whilst ignoring your own issues!

Here we are asking for healing for an aspect of ourselves that has been neglected, rejected or otherwise repressed and unloved. The temptation is to ignore the first aspect that shows up for healing as it may be uncomfortable, however it has shown up for a reason, therefore is time to heal it. Go with the process and be prepared to listen to the guidance that comes through.

Make the Cosmic Connection (page 93).

Scan your being for any part of yourself that you don't like, any place where you do not accept yourself, any part of you that you have tried to ignore, diminish, or disown, any place where you do not respect yourself.

You recognise an aspect of yourself that you've been pushing away. It might be something physical, such as rejection of part of your physical appearance, or it might be something you don't like about your personality, or your behaviour, or your sexuality.

Allow the aspect that is ready for healing to be shown to you. It may be shown symbolically. You might be tempted to push it back down; resist that urge. It is being shown now because you are ready to work on healing and accepting that aspect, however uncomfortable you feel about it in this moment.

Invite the Starbrary light to shine on this aspect of yourself so that it may be blessed and hallowed by the Light. See this aspect lighting up and ask for guidance from your Starbrary and the Star beings on how you can integrate this part of yourself, so that you might come to accept it and love it.

Listen carefully for the response, which may come as words, images, a feeling, or just a kind of knowing. You will get guidance on how to bring this part of yourself into wholeness.

Continue to watch the light flow. Feel your heart chakra becoming wide open, warm and glowing. Imagine it is visibly shining with beautiful Starbrary energy.

Picture yourself standing in front of a full-length mirror. You see your heart chakra shining brightly as you look at yourself. Imagine you are holding your arms out, sending yourself that beautiful heart energy, loving and accepting of all that you are. Know that you are enough already.

Feel yourself bathed in your own heart's energy. You are as worthy of love and acceptance as anybody else. Move towards your reflection, looking deeply into your own eyes, seeing them reflecting the love you bear yourself.

When you are ready thank any Star beings who helped you and the Starbrary quartz. See the beam of light retracting to the star and become aware of being physically present and well-grounded. Hold a grounding stone if you need one and write up your journal.

You can repeat this simple visualisation as many times as you need to until you fully love and accept the whole of yourself.

I shared my own experience of this visualisation with the group. I've had two children, who are now adults, but I still have a 'mummy tummy' which I have felt critical of for years.

Immediately I got told, "Be grateful for your tummy, it sticks out *because* you got pregnant and carried two beautiful children. Love it for that."

Because the Starbraries connect us with Beings of Unity consciousness my experience is that their guidance can come in fast and clear. They cut through our clouded thinking in a no-nonsense, but loving way.

Healing Soulmate Relationships

I used my Tantric Twin Starbrary to do soulmate healing. There is not a hair's breadth between the two crystals until they come to their individual points. Tantric Twin crystals symbolise two people growing in harmony together whilst keeping their individuality.

This visualisation focusses on enhancing the connections formed in loving relationships with our partners, but it could be adapted to harmonise relationships with siblings, parents, or close friends.

Part of the reason we incarnate in soul groups is to help each other grow and develop. That might not always be a comfortable process and sometimes the key lesson is recognising your own self-worth which may be tested by the behaviour of others.

Learning how to be in harmony with yourself is a big lesson which many of us are here to learn. If there is disharmony within you, you will mirror it onto your relationships with others. Equally of course they may project their disharmony onto you. Remember that relationships work both ways.

When we form close relationships with others, we naturally create energy connections. When they are healthy they help us to understand how the other person is thinking and feeling. When we experience difficult times in our relationships these connections may become distorted, stagnated, heavy or draining. Then it is time for a relationship cord clean up.

In my healing practice I specialise in cord release which is an in-depth process and can help you release ties you have to dysfunctional relationships when you need help to let go of their energy. A truly challenging relationship, past or present, is best worked through with the support of an experienced therapist.

Here we will use the Starbrary energy to dissolve any unhealthy cords with a partner whom you love, in order to enhance your relationship. It could be used when you are going through a 'tricky patch', but it is not suitable for use where the relationship has truly broken down.

There should be nothing manipulative about doing this cord clean up as your intention is to harmonise and enhance the energy with someone you already share a close bond with. It is making the effort to do something loving and caring for them, the energy equivalent of cooking them a nice meal, or buying them flowers. If you sense you are coming from a place where you want to 'make' the other person understand you, get them to pay you more attention, or change their behaviour in some other way, then this exercise really isn't appropriate at the moment.

The idea of harmony throughout all our relationships is aspirational for most of us, however you may find you really do experience more harmony as you work with the Starbraries. The truth is you are finding more harmony within yourself which is then mirrored out into your relationships and the wider world.

Although deepening the love that exists between you is the aim of this visualisation not all soulmate relationships are destined to be 'happy ever after'. It is possible that you will choose to leave a relationship if you recognise the dynamic is unhealthy. Sometimes it is more honouring to our integrity to separate from a soul mate. That relationship may have served its purpose in awakening self-respect within you. Soul mate relationships always hold great lessons, even those that do not end in a loving way.

Energy connections form most naturally from chakra to chakra in a loving relationship. For example, heart to heart is very common in a soul mate relationship and helpful for a compassionate and loving connection. Sometimes you will see cords that come from different chakras, for example throat to solar plexus. This is generally less healthy and suggests one partner is dominating, or attempting to control the other, consciously or unconsciously. If you are shown connections which don't seem to be borne of a mutual respect you may want to dissolve them completely, clearing the chakras for healthier connections to form.

In my experience cords rarely connect crown chakra to crown chakra, so I have started the visualisation from the third eye chakra. If however you feel the need to check your crown then go ahead and do so. You may find that there are some chakras without any energy connections. Don't worry about this, it is common for partners to bond more from certain chakras than others. The chakras partners choose to connect from will show something about the nature of their relationship.

For this visualisation holding a Tantric Twin Starbrary would be the ideal, but these are rare crystals. If you don't have one you can hold your Starbrary and put the picture of my Tantric Twin in front of you, or you can access the energy of relationship harmony by holding two similarly sized Starbraries.

Begin by making the Cosmic Connection (page 93)

Now bring your focus to your heart and think about your relationship with your partner. Imagine you are standing opposite your soul mate, face to face. Ask to be shown what the energy connections between you look like. You might see strands of light, cords, or some other connections.

If any of these connections do not look healthy you can invite the Starbrary light to come in and clear away any heaviness or darkness which has been getting in the way of harmony in your relationship. The Starbrary light can dissolve unhealthy connections and clean up heavy energies.

Start by looking at your brow chakra. Check that any connection from your third eye appears bright and flowing. Invite the Starbrary energy to clean up the brow connection if it needs it. Ask that the Starbrary energy helps you achieve a clearer understanding your loved one, so that you might see eye to eye.

Now look at your throat chakra. Check any connection there is bright and flowing. Clean up the energy connection at your throat by inviting the Starbrary light in to dissolve any harshness from your communication with each other. Ask that the Starbrary energy helps you communicate honestly and openly together.

Look at your heart chakra. Check that any connection at your heart is bright and flowing. Invite the Starbrary energy in to cleanse the connection and harmonise the energy. Ask that your heart can be open so that loving energy can flow freely between you.

Check your solar plexus chakra. Is any connection at your solar plexus bright and flowing? Invite the Starbrary light in to dissolve any heaviness or inequality in the connection here. Ask that the Starbrary energy helps you to empower one another.

Look at your sacral chakra. Check any connection at the sacral is bright and flowing. Invite the Starbrary energy to cleanse or dissolve any heaviness here. Ask that you connect in a way that respects each other's desires for touch and sensuality.

Now check your base chakra. Is there a bright and flowing connection here? Invite the Starbrary energy in to cleanse and dissolve any heavy energy. Intend that you will support each other as you navigate the journey of life.

You may feel guided now to go back and check your crown chakra and clean up any connections you find there, or you may be shown any other connections between you that need cleaning up. These are not always chakra to chakra connections. Sometimes you may find connections at the hands, or feet, or elsewhere on the body. Check around your back too. Whenever you find a connection that doesn't look bright and flowing invite the Starbrary energy to cleanse or dissolve it.

When you are happy that all the energy connections between you are light and bright hold your arms out to your soul mate. As you open your arms to them, so they may reach their arms out to you. If they do so then step together and allow yourself to connect chakra to chakra with them in a long and melting hug.

Feel what is like to experience complete harmony between you so that you feel like two people merging into one person; like the Tantric Twin crystal there is no space between you. Enjoy the sense of Oneness with your beloved.

Know you deserve this harmonious connection. Remember to practice forgiveness when your loved one upsets you, or when you upset them. Learning to live and love in harmony with another is one of the reasons you incarnated.

When you release each other and step apart you'll see that you retain your beautiful, glowing connections. You are learning how to be apart and still be in harmonious communion with each other, even at those times when you are physically far away.

Thank your loved one, the Starbrary and any Star beings who helped you. Now allow the light to go back to the star and let the other visions to fade.

You may like to sit in the warm, loving glow for a while before you check your grounding and write up your journal.

Return to this exercise whenever your relationship feels strained or unbalanced. Practicing cord hygiene can be surprisingly helpful in releasing tension within a relationship.

Here is Josie's experience

Wow, that was very deep, loved it. Starbraries never cease to amaze me. I saw the cords, they were washed, they didn't look healthy, but they transformed into the shape of the infinity symbol connecting me to the other person, all clean and shimmering gold. Feel so good now!

Sending Compassion to a Group of People

At the beginning of 2018 I visited the Tucson Gem Show, which is the biggest gem show in the World. Tucson is in Arizona and not far from the border with Mexico. I ate Mexican food, shopped in a Mexican supermarket and could see that the local economy relied on Mexicans in so many ways. I found my dealings with the Mexican people to be friendly and welcoming.

This was in stark contrast to President Trump's assertions that Mexicans were 'rapists and murderers' and his pledge to 'build a wall' to keep them out of the US. It seems utterly bizarre to demonise a whole race of people in this way and to build walls to divide people. I'm old enough to remember the joy and celebration when the Berlin Wall came down!

Just before giving this visualisation for the first time I watched a news clip of the swearing in of a new South African President. It was lovely to watch the hope and optimism with which he was received, his comrades celebrating with singing and dancing. Then the camera panned across to the other side of their parliament where the opposition were sitting stony faced, mostly with their arms tightly crossed. That side of the chamber was predominantly white, the victorious side mostly black. It brought it home to me that even though apartheid has ended in South Africa there is still a huge divide between the black and white communities and a long way to go before there is true integration and mutual respect.

These are just two examples of widespread division in the World, because of prejudice over superficial differences of skin colour, nationality, gender, religion or sexual orientation.

Humanity is still operating from basic tribal programming and it is high time we evolved beyond this! The Starbraries show us there is potential to exist harmoniously. They link to Star beings from differing star systems and yet in them we find a place of unified consciousness and love where there is no separation or exclusion. The Starbraries can help us break down these false barriers and rigid prejudices.

Unity is not an impossible dream. It is the only sane way forward for Humanity. To survive we have to connect, we have to accept, we have to break down prejudice, starting with those who are most receptive to change and allowing that process of change to cascade through the World. As we saw with the Berlin Wall something that seems permanent and rigid can be brought down overnight.

I used the Emergence Starbrary to lead this visualisation as it symbolises a breakthrough into a new way of being.

Make the Cosmic Connection (page 93).

Now bring your attention to your heart centre. Breathing deeply into your heart. See the beautiful Starbrary light opening your heart wide. Knowing that love is always the answer.

Ask the Star beings to help you in finding compassion for your fellow humans. You may be shown a community where there is prejudice, or a place of inequality, or a group of people who are being treated as inferior to others.

The Starbrary light shines out from your heart as pure, unconditional love. No-one is too damaged, or too much of an outsider, to receive the light if they want it.

Imagine those who wish to receive healing opening their arms wide. See them absorbing the beautiful Starbrary light into their hearts. As you watch you may see a transformation happening. Perhaps their expressions look more joyful, or they stand straighter. Maybe their own hearts begin to radiate light to those around them.

When you are ready thank the Starbrary you have been working with and any Star beings who have assisted you. Watch the beam of light return to the star and bring your attention back to your grounding. Pick up a grounding stone if you need one and write up any notes in your journal.

Soothing Mother Earth

This was the first Facebook live visualisation. Steve and I had just come back from a visit to the Ashmolean Museum in Oxford where I was absolutely captivated by a medieval painting, St Nicholas of Bari banishing the Storm by Bicci di Lorenzo (1373–1452). St Nicholas flies from the heavens under a canopy of stars in order to calm a storm over the sea and save the crew of a ship. I kept walking back to gaze at this painting. There seemed to be an immediacy to it, a freshness, despite its great age.

Next day I was due to lead the group's inaugural visualisation and I asked for guidance. On the news I was shown Hurricane Ophelia heading towards the Azores; another in what had been a series of hurricanes. I led the group in a Starbrary visualisation to help calm the storm. When I went back downstairs I found that Steve had bought me a print of the painting at the exact same time I'd been leading the group. I hadn't told him our focus.

This is a short, simple visualisation to send Mother Earth some healing. Although it was originally created for calming a storm, it can be adapted for other turbulent natural events such as earthquakes, fires or volcanic eruptions. As a group we used it to send rain for the fires that burned in the Amazon in 2019 and to send cooling energy for the bush fires raging in Australia at the start of 2020.

Each time we worked there was a positive change reported in the news the following day, whether that was a calming of the winds, rainfall, or cooler temperatures. Many other healers were channelling healing for these areas at the same time, so we are not going to claim all the credit for our work with the Starbraries, but I am convinced we helped.

For the first session I set my altar with a dove feather to represent peace. My focus was to soothe Mother Earth's ruffled feathers.

First make the Cosmic Connection (page 93).

Feel the Starbrary light flowing through you and ask for the energy of Peace to descend upon you. You experience a deeply peaceful vibration flowing through your whole being.

Peace flows out from your heart chakra to spread a calming blanket of energy across the Planet. See the calming energy soothing Mother Earth's turbulent emotions.

Focus now on the storm that is brewing. Ask that the energy of Peace is sent to the storm. Trust that it will flow to the places where it is most needed. See the energy calming the winds, soothing the seas, defusing the tension and bringing a sense of deep peace to the Earth.

Remember that you can be a channel for Peace on our beautiful Planet.

When you are ready you thank the Starbrary and let the beam of light go back to the star. Pick up a grounding stone if you need one and write up your journal.

You could leave your Starbrary on your altar with the candle lit (providing it is safe to do so) with the intention that peaceful energy continues to be sent to the troubled area. For safety make sure you snuff the flame out before you leave the house or go to bed.

If you adapt the visualisation allow yourself to be guided to send the most harmonious energy. For example we were inspired to send cooling energy to Australia for the fires, not rain. At the time lots of other healers on social media were calling for rain to be sent; it was no doubt well intended but unfortunately Australia was hit with devastating flooding! Following your higher guidance will lead to better results.

Here is Lisa's feedback from the visualisation we did for the Amazon rainforest:

I kept being 'told' to just relax and let the healing energy through. Started to hear a thundering noise and felt/saw a huge waterfall - I knew my energy was at one with the waterfall and flowing through this. I had to keep letting this happen - my heart was aching and it was a really pure white light. I kept feeling/knowing all I had to do was keep this connection and let my energy flow with and through the waterfall into the grid. The noise of the waterfall, the thundering of the water was coming and going and my starbrary was pulsating in my hand. Towards the end I could feel/see the most beautiful place - foliage, trees, lush, birds, insect sounds and a soft light filtering through and always the sound of the waterfall.

Sometimes the Starbraries have their own ideas about where their energy is needed most. If it feels okay just go with it. Here is what Sherille reported after the original visualisation:

I was directed to place my 3 Starbraries in an equilateral triangle...I sat in the triangle and although I had already grounded and protected myself, did so again with you and then opened the connection. This was where I lost you!

I was sitting palms up with my DT in my lap when my crown just exploded open, the energy was so strong and " bigger " than I expected. I was both happy and tearful at the same time because the healing and love was so unbelievably powerful flooding through me.

I tried to focus the energy on the hurricane Ophelia but it was too small an area. I saw the planet and the energy was like a fog covering the entire planet, at first creeping like fingers

114

over the oceans, mountains, through the forests and cities growing ever thicker until all I could see was a white ball. I was aware that the energy was also flowing into the centre of the Earth as well and heard the healing will come from within ourselves as well.

I saw the energy coursing through the grid I was shown in my first meditation with them and then on through the networks we discovered on the Golden Healer day, right around, through, above and beyond the Earth, strengthening the Earth's connection to the Cosmos and the help offered.

The energy kept coming in waves, eventually when it lessened, I had heard you say we could direct energy to a personal site and I asked for help and protection for the first generation redwoods, some of whom are 1500 - 2000 years old, which are in danger from the fires spreading in N. California.

I was called upon to raise my arms to the heavens, rather like the image on your book cover (Light behind the Angels) *except I was sitting, not only was the energy coming from my palms but also shooting out of my wrists in straight lines, unbelievably strong and lasted some time after you closed. I stopped the healing myself, or I could have been there all night, and used mahogany obsidian and kiwi jasper to ground myself and drank some water. It wasn't enough! I needed to be outside.*

I had been directed to erect an altar in the garden a while back so sat next to it. We'd had a very wet and windy day but now the sky was completely clear, not a single cloud, the wind only in the treetops, and so many stars (we have light pollution and stars can be sparse) but that night was incredible. I was watching one very bright star which suddenly disappeared, then reappeared, then after a while disappeared again.

115

We do have planes flying to and from the US which pass high overhead and I thought it was probably one of those, but there were no navigation lights and it wasn't moving. I watched for about five minutes and then it went for good but sensed the ETs had made themselves known to let me know they were aware of what we were doing and how pleased they were.

The " star " was sitting between the first and second stars in the handle of the Ursa Major constellation, very precise. I've looked it up and found that the 3 stars marking the handle represent the 3 mourning maidens, and the remaining stars represent the bier or bowl. I used 3 crystals, could the earth be the bier? I don't know, maybe I'm just being fanciful.

I stayed outside until I started to get cold and came in. My cat always flops on my thigh and cuddles as soon as I sit down which he automatically did then shot up as if he'd been electrocuted. He tried again several times, but the residual energy was just too strong for him.

Sometimes only a hug will do!

A Healing Circle for Mother Earth

It is time that all those who have been awakened pay attention to healing our Planet. She has been taken for granted for too long and the signs of her stress are obvious. The Starbraries made it clear from our first meeting that they have emerged at this pivotal point in our history to help us through the changes to come.

Attending a local Women's Circle meeting in July 2019 our focus was on Home, both our personal homes and our collective home on Earth. When I was prompted to hear what Mother Earth had to say I was startled. I heard her loudly and clearly say, "Help!" I wondered whether I was being melodramatic, but when our Circle leader gave her feedback she had experienced exactly the same clear plea.

I continued to dialogue with Earth Mother. She said, "Why are you doing this to me when I have given you everything?" I went on to channel golden healing to her.

I've been concerned about the environment for as long as I can remember. When I was just a little girl, I would become very upset about the destruction of the rainforests. That was almost 50 years ago. 50 years of continued deforestation is almost too upsetting to contemplate.

As a Green Party activist in my twenties people looked at me askance for promoting recycling. Now recycling has become mainstream and people are much more aware of issues with plastics, so there is a shift happening.

These days I aim to be a thoughtful consumer and to buy the most ethical version of products I can find and afford, Fairtrade, rainforest friendly, low food miles and so on. I

117

know these are small contributions in the grand scheme of things, but if we each make our small changes they will add up to large scale change.

We are now in a global environmental crisis, entering a phase of mass extinction and most politicians are still tinkering around at the edges of the issues. Some are even denying there is a problem. I am reminded of the legendary Nero fiddling whilst Rome burns!

We all need to do what we can to help and we need to do it now. As well as taking practical steps in the physical world why not commit to be a channel for healing the Earth? Follow through as often as you can manage. Any healing you offer for the Earth is valuable.

I was inspired to create a Starbrary group visualisation for healing Mother Earth as a result of my experience at the Women's Circle. When I asked which Starbrary wanted to work with me the Manifestation Starbrary made itself known.

The Manifestation Starbrary contains a smaller crystal point within the larger crystal. Incredible coloured light shines off the inner crystal. I can't show this in black and white for obvious reasons, but there is an intense electric blue, a brilliant magenta and a bright gold.

This crystal has been dedicated for Earth healing. The inner crystal forms a sanctuary space where we can connect. The visualisation still worked for members of the Starbrary Custodians Facebook group afterward when they were listening in and following the instructions 'alone'. As linear time is an illusion on some level our healing ritual is still happening and you can join us.

Looking at the Manifestation Starbrary and holding a Starbrary of your own should be enough to connect you to our Starbrary Circle's Earth healing. If the door in the crystal doesn't open for you it isn't the right time for you to enter. Don't try to force the door. Do some healing work on yourself first and then try again.

Manifestation Starbrary Quartz

First make the Cosmic Connection (page 93)

See yourself standing in the Starbrary light. Know you are a pillar of Light. Imagine the Manifestation Starbrary as a huge crystal standing in front of you. It is accessible to those who have done their Starbrary Connection and are ready to serve.

From whichever direction you are connecting a doorway will open in the Manifestation Starbrary. You walk inside the crystal and the door closes behind you. As you walk into the crystal you feel lighter and realise you are standing in your Light body. Any heaviness has been left on the outside, nothing impure can accompany those who enter here.

You are inside the beautiful clear outer crystal and in front of you there is another crystal, a crystal within a crystal. You may sense the others who are already here, also in their Light bodies.

Inside the inner crystal there is an incredible concentration of light. When you feel ready you walk into that second chamber, the central crystal. As you step in you see beams of brilliant gold, brilliant blue and brilliant magenta filling the space. Bathe in this incredible light and absorb whichever of these colours you need most at this time.

Now you see the others who are standing in a circle. They make a space for you and you take your place. You are part of a unified circle of healers within this sacred space of Light. As you join hands with those beside you the colours become more intense, brighter still. You join the group's intention to send as much healing for Mother Earth as you can safely channel at this time.

You see that a cone of brilliant energy has formed above the circle. This cone of beautiful healing energy is being created by the group. The energy is swirling and streaming outwards through the point of the inner crystal and then out again through the point of the outer crystal. You are aware that this healing energy is being sent out across the Earth. Watch the beautiful Light as it streams out to bathe the whole Planet in Light.

You continue to hold hands in the sacred circle, sending your heartfelt gratitude to your Earth Mother. She has given you everything. You breathe her air, you walk upon her body, she provides you with shelter and food. You enjoy her bounty and you feel the deepest gratitude for her generosity. You send her your love and respect. Continue to send her healing energy, allowing it to intensify as you become used to this frequency of Light.

Once you feel you have sent enough healing for the time being you give the hands you are holding a squeeze, acknowledging that this has been a group effort, true teamwork. You release the others' hands.

You turn to walk back out from the inner crystal, back into the cool clear energy of the outer crystal. Now you walk out of the crystal, stepping back through the doorway into your own space. The door of the outer crystal closes behind you. You know the door will open again for you when you are ready to send more healing for Mother Earth.

Let the Starbrary beam of light go back to its star. Allow yourself a quiet moment to settle. Hold a grounding stone if you need to and write up your journal.

Wow, such powerful energy! I saw a formation of stars and planets making a huge star in the sky that was beaming out healing, not just to earth but the entire universe. It was incredible. Then saw all of us in this group in a circle sending out light. Feel very moved by it. Thank you Lauren

Josie

Thank you Lauren that was amazing. I was aware that we were all beacons connected to the network that runs through and around the planet, each of us radiating the energy in all directions to all beings animate and inanimate, I was especially aware of the tree people who danced with the energy. A powerful and beautiful session. Sherille

Lisa used the visualisation after the live broadcast and found it was still potent:

HOT beyond anything!! The energy was incredible. Able to access into the Starbrary and get deeper into it - the light was pulsating quite rapidly, really beautiful, beautiful pink/magenta/gold edged - as we moved in and held hands the energy was so intense and the heat - my own starbrary was so hot in my hand. I felt/heard a massive sigh - felt very emotional, tearful, in awe but safe and connected. So powerful - the pink/magenta was sparking and pulsating and then evened out and the colour was white and iridescent, calmer, ebbing and flowing, in and out, very tranquil. Able to pull out and leave starbrary - very, very calm, beautiful. Amazing Lauren, thank you - feeling very energized for the day - I have a presentation later with work so feeling super powerful now, think that massive sigh came from Mother Earth... xx

Supporting the Earth's Energy Grid

There are energy channels forming a network across the Earth very like the meridian channels we have in our bodies. Some people see these as a geometric grid around the Planet, others speak of them in terms of energy lines such as ley lines, or dragon lines.

In ancient times our ancestors were more aware of Earth energy lines and sited their most important structures, such as stone circles or places of worship upon them. It was the alignment of old mounds, churches, standing stones and other archaeological features that alerted the Victorian Alfred Watkins to the existence of ley lines which he wrote about in his classic book The Old Straight Track.

I believe that human activity has disrupted and depleted some of these energy pathways. I don't mean digging in your garden, I'm talking about industrial drilling operations such as those used in drilling for oil, or for fracking. Deep excavations, such as open cast mining and large scale construction are likely to cause breaks and blockages in the energy lines.

Innovations such as wind turbines are potentially useful, cutting down pollution and global warming, but when sited insensitively they may cause disruption for Earth's energy. As with the meridians in our bodies if the energy flow is broken or blocked then the rest of that line may become stagnated and unhealthy.

I believe we can feed healing energy into depleted parts of the grid and that as we work with the Starbraries we may also receive guidance on healing the grid where it has been damaged.

First make the Cosmic Connection (page 93)

Know that you are always connected with Earth and she with you. Your Earth Mother deserves gratitude for all the gifts she has provided you with. Every mouthful of food, each breath that you breathe, your very body. You are as much part of the Earth as any tree, animal or crystal.

Mother Earth supplies all your needs and in return you can gift her with the healing energy you channel. Focus now on the Earth at your feet and notice it is glowing with the energy that you are channelling. See the Starbrary energy flowing into the Earth.

As you watch the energy is shining brighter and clearer, radiating out from where you stand. See the bright energy spreading across the landscape like a web or a grid.

You may be shown places where the energy lines have been damaged or disconnected. Ask for guidance on whether you can help to heal that damage and allow yourself to be shown how.

Know that as you radiate healing energy from where you stand countless other people are doing the same. As more healers plug in and channel energy for the Earth the whole Earth grid will become brighter and more energised.

The more of us who feed Mother Earth's Grid the stronger and more vibrant it will become. You can feed healing energy into the Earth Grid every day if you want to.

Once you feel you have channelled enough for today thank the Starbrary and allow the beam of light to go back to the star until next time.

You probably will feel quite grounded as you've been connecting into the Earth, but pick up a grounding stone if you need one and write up your notes in your journal.

Sherille has been shown the Earth's grid in some detail. This is her the account of her second visit to the Starbrary Crystal Cave:

I swam down into the ocean to the glorious garden and placed my starbrary in the centre. It began to grow and I entered it and travelled upwards until I was again sitting in the middle of the lotus. The star beings once again channelled the Light through my crown chakra and it was very strong. I could feel it entering the Earth and coursing through the grid.

I was aware that the Light would be experienced by everything in and on the Planet. The grid has a very fine 'mesh' in contact with the surface of the Planet and every creature that walks on the surface receives the Light, likewise the creatures in the water, which is in contact with the underlying mesh. The creatures of the air are not forgotten. Each plant and tree received the Light through its roots and when an airborne creature lands on one of these they also receive the Light.

Healing the Earth from Space

16th July 2019 was a Full Moon and a partial eclipse, which felt significant. It also marked the 50th anniversary of Man first walking on the Moon. I hadn't realised this when I chose the date for a Starbrary live visualisation.

The anniversary made me reflect on those familiar pictures of Planet Earth taken from Space. The ability of Mankind to go into orbit and gain a higher perspective on our home planet has happened within just one human lifetime. From Space we can see how exquisitely beautiful she is.

We can use this elevated perspective to unite and send Mother Earth healing. Now that really would be a small step for man and a giant leap for Mankind!

Begin by making the Cosmic Connection (page 93)

You are aware of the beam of Starbrary light directly above you. As you put your focus on the beam you feel yourself being transported straight upwards within the starry light. You are lifted out of Earth's atmosphere and find you are looking down upon our beautiful blue planet from space.

As you look upon the Earth you sense her place within the Universe, a part of the Cosmic whole. Earth is a special place. Know that her cries for help have been heard and are being answered. Feel the love that is being beamed to her from many places in the Universe at this time.

You are part of a larger tribe of healers. Know that you are connected to this larger healing movement even when you are working alone. You send Starbrary light down to the Earth and see it bathing the Planet.

Viewing the Earth from Space you make a commitment to help in whatever way you are guided. You choose to do one thing for the Earth that you know you can honour. Your pledge truly is a small step for man, but a giant leap for mankind. When enough of us take these small steps, mankind will make a giant leap and we will become worthy custodians of the Planet.

When you are ready you travel back down through the Starbrary beam, back into Earth's atmosphere and firmly back into your body. Thank the Starbrary and any Star beings who helped you. Allow the beam of Starbrary energy to go back to the star and ensure you are fully grounded, picking up a grounding stone if you need one. Write your experiences in your journal, including the commitment you made as a reminder to follow through.

127

The Three Wishes:

A Gift from your Starbrary Godmother

I was inspired to create the Three Wishes Visualisation for New Year's Eve 2018. The God Janus, for whom January is named, is shown with two faces, one that looks back and one that looks forward.

I have found New Year's Eve to be an auspicious time for spiritual work (before partaking of alcohol of course) because it is symbolic of a fresh start. Any day can be a fresh start, but the New Year feels particularly significant, probably because so many people are celebrating across the Globe.

You don't need to wait for the New Year to do the Three Wishes visualisation. Other dates may be more meaningful for you, such as the Chinese New Year, or your own birthday, which is your personal Solar Return.

Before you set any new intentions, or claim your wishes, you will be reviewing the year that has just passed and asking your Starbraries and the Star beings to assist you in seeing your life and your challenges from a higher perspective. It is easy to get enmeshed in the drama of life and fail to notice the larger patterns and lessons which are opportunities for spiritual growth. These lessons may become apparent further down the line, but you often need help to gain the insights at the time.

Once you have gathered the insights you can release any angst, stress and tension connected with those situations so that you are ready to walk through the energetic doorway without carrying all your old issues with you. You are totally permitted to put your heavy baggage down and walk through the gateway unburdened. You can claim your fresh start.

Remember a large part of the Starbrary Mission appears to be about raising our personal vibration so that we may in turn help others to raise theirs. Carrying the weight of your past will drag your energy down and make you less effective as a healer. You owe it to everyone to lighten up.

You will also be counting your blessings, because even in the most difficult years positive things happen. I'm encouraging you to identify and appreciate the good stuff. I do believe there is a virtuous circle and the more you count your blessings and feel thankful the more you are given to feel thankful for.

The more beauty, love and positivity you feed your mind with the more you will begin to look for the best in everything. This doesn't make you into a 'Pollyanna' but it does make you feel happier than dwelling primarily on the angst and the trials of life.

You will be making wishes for the New Year ahead. One for yourself, one for your Community, whether that is your family, your friends, your neighbours, or a group you belong to and one for the Earth. You don't need to plan your wishes in advance; allow yourself to be inspired by the Starbrary energy.

This is a longer visualisation than usual so make sure you give yourself all the time you need.

Have pen and paper to hand and your chosen Starbrary quartz crystal.

First make the Cosmic Connection (page 93)

As you sit in the beautiful Starbrary light ask to be given a higher perspective on events from the year that has just gone by. Imagine turning the pages of a calendar backwards as you review your year. Some months may turn lightly and easily, other months may feel heavier and may contain events where you need to pause and look at what happened in more detail.

Keep looking at the events of the last year from a higher perspective. Don't get involved in the emotional drama, stay in alignment with the Starbrary energy.

As you review the events from this higher level of consciousness it may become apparent why you had to go through that experience. If you can't see why ask for assistance from the Star beings. Listen carefully for their answer which may come as words, images, or feelings.

Now ask to release any heavy emotions relating to that situation, including anger, grief, hurt, or a lack of forgiveness. Release as much of the angst as you can. You will see the brilliant light of the Starbrary dissolving heavy or cloudy energies as you work through them.

Take your time with this process; it is important that you leave as much of your old baggage behind as possible so that you do not carry it forward into the year ahead.

Keep moving through your calendar, continuing to pause wherever difficult situations occurred, examining them from a higher perspective, asking for help where necessary and listening to the answers, before cleansing away the old energy with the help of your Starbrary. Work through this process until you feel you have released as much as you can.

Now you are going to look back again over your year. This time you are looking for those things you can be grateful for, the events that lifted your heart, the kindnesses of others, the celebrations and achievements. Look at all the things you have done that have been positive or kind, that have given you a warm glow, or a feeling of satisfaction. Take the time to realise that as challenging as your year may have been, some genuinely heart-warming and positive things happened too. Spend as long as you want, reviewing each month and appreciating all the gifts the year has given you.

You can see a glowing doorway of Light ahead of you, the portal into the New Year. Now you see you have a Starbrary Godmother standing beside the doorway. She is going to be granting you three wishes for the year ahead. You will make one wish for yourself, one for your community and one wish for the Earth.

Your wishes absolutely can come true so don't limit yourself. Let your Starbrary and the Star beings guide you so that you make your wishes with integrity, in alignment with your life purpose and for the highest good of all they will touch.

Write your three wishes down and hone them until you feel really happy with them. Know that you will be walking through the doorway of the coming year carrying these bright intentions with you.

Think about how good these wishes will feel when they come true. Holding your Starbrary, knowing you are connected with a source of incredible power, you declare your wish for yourself, either out loud or in your mind. Notice how uplifted you feel by your wish. You may sense a warm glow of supportive energy coming in which will help to make your wish manifest for you. Allow yourself to feel that your wish is already coming to pass, it isn't going to take a whole year to manifest. Your wish is already starting to become your reality as you prepare to walk through the doorway into the New Year.

Now make your wish for your Community. Declare your wish out loud, or in your mind, and allow the light of the Starbrary to infuse the wish with light. Sense how wonderful this wish will be when it manifests, how good it will feel when you see it come into being. Visualise the people your wish will touch looking radiantly happy.

Now make your third wish, your wish for the World. Declare your wish out loud or in your mind and allow the Starbrary energy to energise your intention. See the Starbrary energy spreading out across the whole World, bringing radiant Light down onto the Planet.

Now your Starbrary Godmother waves her magic wand over your head, covering you with sparkling energy. You take a deep breath and step through the glowing doorway into the New Year carrying your bright intentions with you.

When you are ready to close back down say thank you to your Starbrary, your Starbrary Godmother and any Star beings and then allow the beam of starry energy to go back to the star. Ground yourself, pick up a grounding stone if you need one and make your notes in your journal before joining any New Year celebrations.

I received the following feedback from Monika at the end of January 2019:

This was only the third starbrary meditation I had done with you and I wasn't expecting too much. The other two had been peaceful experiences. This one blew my socks off! All three of my wishes have already happened. I felt so peaceful and fulfilled after the visualisation that I decided not to go out on New Year's Eve as we'd planned to.

The next morning it was beautiful sunny weather. I'd made a wish to start doing more healing for the Earth. My husband and I went out and we walked for hours next to the canal. We noticed a forest and went inside. We could see about 200 trees had been marked for cutting down. I said to my husband, "I have to do some work. I have to speak to each of these trees to let them know they need to retrieve their energies." Some I hugged and some I touched and my husband helped me. I felt so fulfilled.

We watched a beautiful sunset together. He felt peaceful and happy and we both slept like logs. We've never felt better – it was like the trees were healing us as well. Nothing could touch me in my work and his work was stress free for several weeks. That was something that he hadn't experienced in a long, long time.

We have been reminded of the saying, "You cannot change the World around you, but you can change how you react."

My other two wishes were more personal and have also come true, but I wanted to share this Earth healing wish as it manifested the very next day and felt so incredible.

Chapter Six

Starbrary Layouts and Grids

I've loved the stars too fondly to be fearful of the night.

Galileo Galilei

The Cosmic Infusion

This layout is deceptively simple: place a Starbrary crystal on each of your main chakras. The intention is to infuse your chakric column with Starbrary light. Place each crystal with the point facing downwards to direct the Starbrary light as it comes in.

Add a large grounding crystal, or several smaller grounding crystals, such as hematite, to the Earth Star chakra which is an off the body, or transpersonal, chakra located between and below your feet. This will not only help you stay grounded but it will also assist in channelling the Starbrary energy through you and down into the Earth.

If you have enough Starbraries you may also add one for the Soul Star, a transpersonal chakra located about 12 inches above your crown. The Soul Star acts like a natural transformer for cosmic energy, moderating it so that you are not overwhelmed. A final Starbrary can be placed for the Stellar Gateway, a transpersonal chakra located at the top of your aura about as far as you can reach with your hand above your head. This is the point at which cosmic energy enters your personal energy field.

Ten minutes in this layout should be plenty, but you can lie in it for longer if you are enjoying the experience. When you have finished sit up slowly and have a drink of water. Make some notes in your journal and ensure you have come around properly before you get on with your day.

I wouldn't recommend this layout for newcomers to the Starbraries as it is potentially very strong!

The Starbrary Compass

The Starbrary Compass was inspired by an experience of getting a bit lost. Steve and I were exploring a forest that was new to us. We followed a path, but we didn't have a map or compass to guide us. When the path branched we took a track that looked like it would loop us back around to our starting place. Needless to say it didn't and we ended up miles from where we had set out! We decided the next time we went exploring that we would carry a compass.

On our forest adventure we'd started in nice sunny weather, chatting to each other and not really paying attention to where we were going. Once we realised we were lost the Sun had gone behind clouds, it was chilly and it looked like it might rain. Life can be very similar; we wander blithely along without paying much attention until suddenly we realise we have wandered off track and things aren't looking so good.

I have a little brass compass my daughter bought me. I keep it in my study where it reminds symbolically me to stay focussed and to check that I am heading in the right direction on my life path.

Using a compass layout with the Starbraries seemed appropriate and confirmation came through quickly in an email from an artist who was making a stained glass compass for our front door. She sent me a photo of the work in process. I hadn't heard anything from her in months so I took that as a positive sign.

This layout is about working with our Starbraries to help us keep a clear direction so that we don't end up wandering off course, or taking unnecessary diversions.

You'll need four or five Starbrary quartz crystals. Use four Starbraries placed around you in alignment with the cardinal points of the compass, points facing outwards to the North, South, East and West. Check with a physical compass if you aren't sure which direction your meditation space faces. There are compass apps for phones these days if you don't own a compass. Just make sure you take your phone out of your meditation space before you start meditating.

You can sit on a chair, or on a cushion on the floor, for this exercise. Face the direction you feel you need to connect with most at this time:

East: If you are at the start of something new, or you would like fresh inspiration, it is morning, or you are connecting in the Springtime.

South: If you need an infusion of power, you need the energy and enthusiasm to grow a project, it is afternoon, or in the Summer.

West: If you are ready to harvest the fruits of your labours, you need to appreciate what you already have, it is evening, or Autumn.

North: If you need to rest, you need to honour an ending, you need to release something, it is Night, or Winter.

If you have a fifth Starbrary you can hold this at your heart centre. Make sure you are firmly grounded and add grounding stones under your seat if you need them.

As you sit in meditation notice the energy of the four directions and be particularly aware of the direction you are facing. You may ask for support from each of the directions.

Sense the directions helping you to be centred and aligned to your life purpose.

Affirm your intention to be of service in bringing Light down to the Planet. Acknowledge that sometimes you get distracted from your purpose and may wander off track. Ask that you will be reminded to realign to your inner compass, and that you will allow your Starbrary compass to bring you back on track, over and over, as often as you need it.

When you have finished check you are still grounded and write up any notes in your journal.

The Starbrary Diamond Net

You can lie in a Starbrary Diamond Net for stress release and personal healing. Use four Starbraries. Place a Starbrary an arm's reach above your head, one the same distance below your feet and the other two at each side of you at waist level at the distance your arms would reach if they were stretched out. Start with the points facing outwards to release pain and tension. Once you feel more relaxed turn the points inwards to recharge and invigorate.

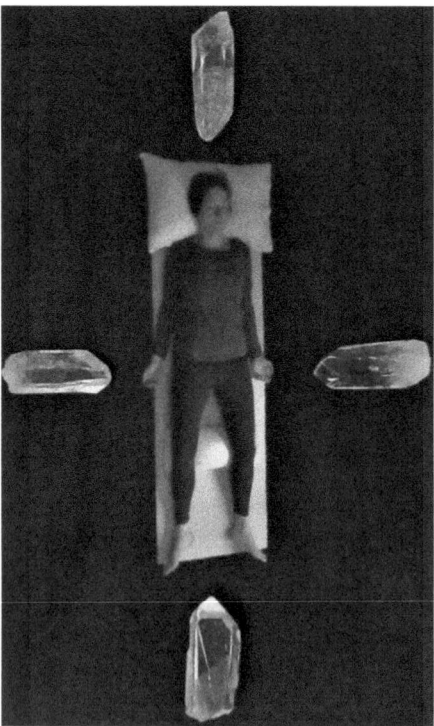

Lie back and relax and let the Starbraries do their work. 10 – 20 minutes is normally plenty of time for a layout like this. You can repeat the Net regularly if you want.

Set the intention that you will come out of the Net at the optimum time, or set a timer if you think you'll fall asleep. When you sit up hold a grounding stone if you need one and write up any notes in your journal.

The Starbrary Star Net

A seven-pointed star with elongated points is called an elven star. The seven points invoke the energy of the Pleiades, or Seven Sisters.

This net brings you into contact with transpersonal energy. It is helpful for observing your actions and life situations from a higher, more detached viewpoint.

You can place yourself in a Starbrary Star Net by lying on a black cloth and placing seven Starbrary quartz crystals around you to create the seven points of the elven star. Before the Starbraries came along we used Herkimer Diamonds to create the Star Net, which worked well. Starbraries are even better!

Place the Starbraries pointing inwards towards you. Place one above your head and one below each foot, lying with your legs comfortably apart. Place a Starbrary each side of your shoulders and on each side of your hips to complete the elven star shape.

Lie in the Starbrary net for 10-20 minutes. You may want to play some soft relaxing music. Don't choose anything with a strong beat that could distract you.

Imagine you are in the Universe being bathed in twinkling starlight. You may find you gain insight into your creations so far and you may be inspired to uplift your manifestations to a higher level. Know that you are making your contribution to the song of the Universe.

When you are ready to come out sit up and hold a grounding stone if you need one. Write up any notes in your journal.

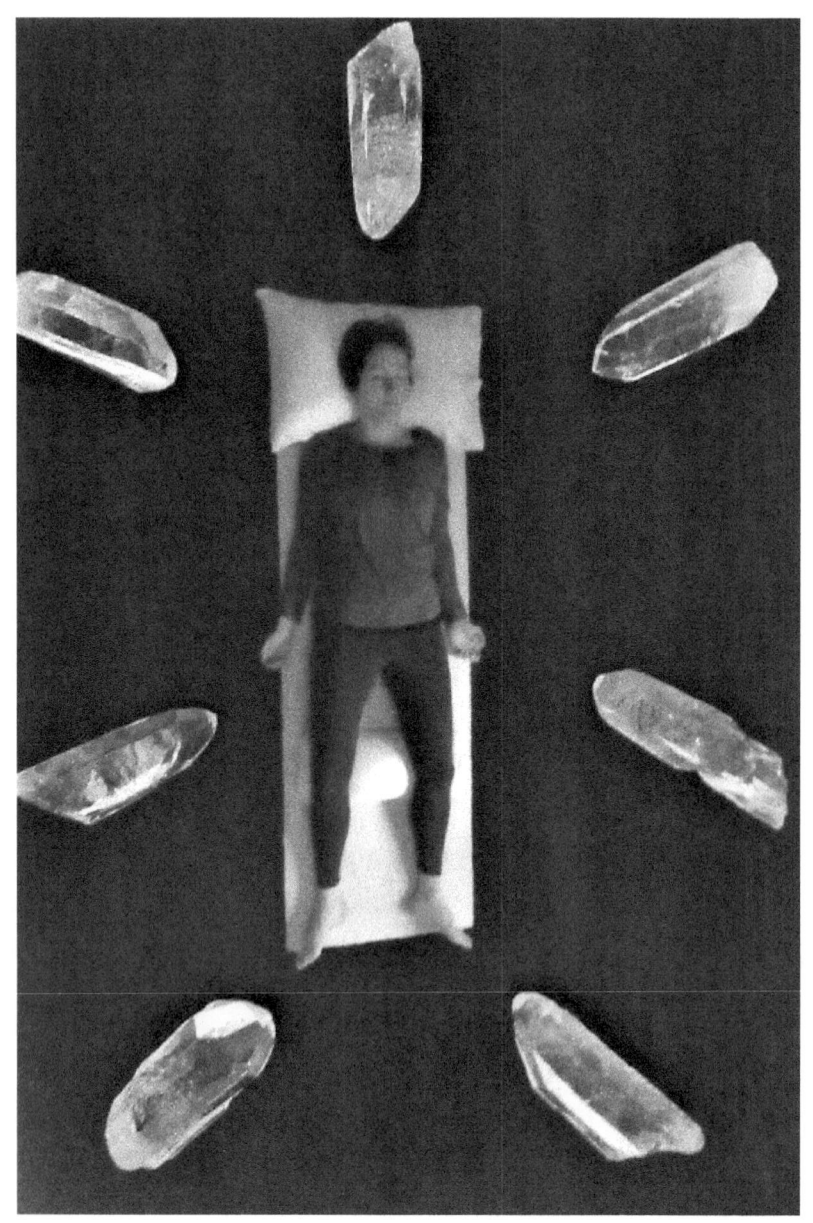

Sending Starbrary Healing with the Elven Star

Steve made me this beautiful healing plate some years ago. The base is wood, with an elven star made from twisted copper wire and a seven-pointed star in the centre from beaten copper. The crystals are mounted on small copper posts which angle them into the centre. I exchanged the original quartz crystals for seven small Starbrary quartz, choosing channeler and transmitter Starbraries for the job.

The plate makes it easy to send Starbrary healing to a place or a person (with their consent). I put a map of the area, or a photo of the person, on the central copper star. It can be used with a central larger Starbrary to gather the combined energies of the seven Starbraries and send the healing to the intended recipient.

143

A plain copper disk, or a mirror, could be substituted for the base, on which you could arrange your seven Starbraries in the star shape.

If you don't use copper wires to form the star you can make the energetic connections between the Starbraries by tracing an Elven star using a larger Starbrary point with the intention of making the shape energetically.

The diagram overleaf shows how to draw an Elven Star with a continuous line. Starting at point 1 move your crystal point with intention in the direction indicated by the arrows. You can imagine a beam of bright white Starbrary light flowing from your crystal point as you trace the star.

Make sure you have done your grounding and protection before you start to send any healing. When you have finished sending the healing detach from the person or place.

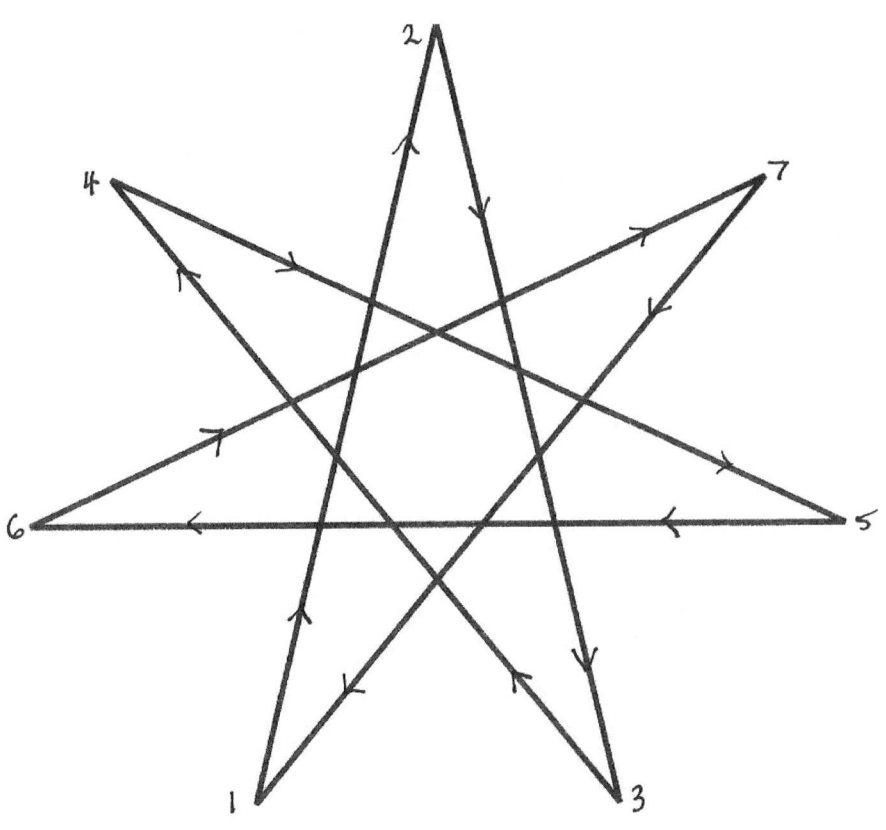

Using Starbraries with Metatron's Cube

Metatron's Cube is a symbol of sacred geometry which I particularly enjoy working with. You can use Metatron's Cube as a focus for manifestation because it contains within it the shapes of all the Platonic Solids, which are believed to be the sacred geometrical building blocks of Creation.

Use the power of this symbol wisely and with the caveat, "May this be for the highest good of all." Adding this phrase helps to protect us from inadvertently allowing our egos to take control and making selfish choices.

I place a focus for the energy in the centre of Metatron's Cube, whether that is a central crystal, a photo, or a symbolic object. Then I place the Starbrary crystals intuitively around, building the grid until it feels right. I usually keep it very simple. You can visualise lines of light connecting each crystal on the grid so that they form a glowing web of light.

A Starbrary Grid for Unity

I created this grid using Metatron's Cube ahead of a meeting I was chairing. I was aware that we had a lot of work to get through and that some members of the group had strongly differing opinions about how to proceed. The intention of the grid was to unify our purpose in putting the best interests of our Organisation ahead of individual agendas.

There were six people attending so I chose six Starbraries to represent the individuals. I arranged them using a Seal of Solomon layout and I pointed them inwards to a larger Starbrary which symbolised us coming together to work for a common purpose. I visualised us listening to each other respectfully and working in harmony.

You could set up a similar grid for unity in a group. Ideally match the number of Starbraries to the people involved and arrange them in a balanced geometrical shape.

Creating your own Layouts and Grids

You may be inspired to create your own layouts or grids with your Starbraries. If you feel guided to try them out and see what happens. Keep notes of your experiments in your journal.

Here is Nicola's story – proving that spirituality can be fun!

Last time I did a meditation with my two starbraries (it was one of Lauren's starbrary circles) they kept insisting they needed more companions. I checked with Lauren and she said she would be bringing them to the Diploma level next May – this would be the next time I would see her. A few days later I saw on FB that she had sourced some more and some were ready to go to new homes already. Lauren showed them on FB and I was immediately drawn to one large one and a set of 4 small ones (I might have yelled "OMG that's Arcturus!" on seeing the big one), and so they came to live with me (my first two starbraries were sat on my altar looking slightly smug at this point).

*Soooo, when the package arrived, it turns out the Quads had become Quins, and the 5 of them were fizzing away, nattering to each other and to anyone who was willing to listen. So I now have 8 (**EIGHT**!) starbraries. Today I did an unguided meditation with the Quins – henceforth known as The Rockette-eers (It was originally The Rockettes, but they wanted it tweaked). This is what happened in that meditation:*

I laid down with the Rockette-eers. One was on my crown, one at each temple under a sweatband and one each in my hands held points towards my head. There was also a petrified wood at my earth star.

As soon as I laid down, I had that feeling on my body you get when you are travelling fast – a pressure or resistance, like my skin was being drawn back. When I started the meditation, I was immediately drawn straight up, flying towards the stars and as I went up, one got brighter and bigger – I got the sense it was a portal and I went through it into darkness. It took me a few minutes to realise I was riding on a comet. It was very small, the size of a motorbike or a jet ski, and that's how I was riding it. It didn't have handlebars, just a dorsal fin like a dolphin to hold onto – so it's my space Dolphin. It took me to Andromeda first. We landed and I got off the Dolphin and walked around. There were no people there which was strange, then I realised if I concentrated, I could see them but they were translucent like ghosts. I realised I wasn't here on Andromeda to do anything, rather I was being shown how the Dolphin worked. So, back to the Dolphin I went and climbed on. It tipped back and with a tremendous burst of energy took off. We went back to outer space. Where shall we go next? I know! The Pleiades!

We zoomed through space, tipping like a motorbike does around bends, curving around the stars of the Pleiades, until we landed on a planet. I got off and had a quick look around then returned to the Dolphin. We took off again – where next? Arcturus! And off we zoomed. Much the same as before I got off and had a quick look around before returning to the Dolphin. Off we went – where next? I asked for Sirius, but nope. I'm not sure why not but I jokingly said to myself I don't have a starbrary that connects there and then realised I was probably right and I can foresee more starbraries in my future... Ai (facepalm... what have I started?!?!). So, I let the Dolphin decide where we were going next (not that I'm really in charge of it).

We zipped along and came to Pluto (which will always be a planet in my heart). We whizzed around Pluto, waved at Charon and then Chiron in the distance, then got to Uranus and the Neptune (wrong order, but I guess Uranus was closer to Pluto). Then we swooped past Saturn and dipped through its rings, we swung past Jupiter and then swung round Mars (I'm surprised I didn't get seasick). I waved at Earth as we bypassed it and went to Venus. We dipped down into the Venusian atmosphere – apparently I needed some lovely Venus energy as we floated there for a while. Then we made a quick whistle-stop tour of Mercury, the Sun and the Moon as we flew into the white portal and I was back on Earth.

I'm not sure if the Rockette-eers will tell me where they connect – if they even connect to specific stars. They felt like they were surfing the webs between my other 3 starbraries, like Navigators, which is an interesting thought (OMG now I'm in Flight of the Navigator).

Nicola

Chapter Seven

Joining with Others

Between death and a new birth, we know that our body,
down to its smallest particles, is formed out of the cosmos.
For we ourselves prepare this physical body, bringing
together in it the whole of animal nature;
we ourselves build it.

Rudolf Steiner

Joining with Others

Whether we have connected with the Starbraries in a workshop, at a Retreat, in a class, or in the Starbrary Custodians Facebook group, I have a sense of Unity within the group. I believe this is because the Star beings who encoded these crystals are evolved to a level where they naturally co-operate with each other and join forces for the highest good.

As humans it makes a refreshing change to feel we are united and working together without adversarial or competitive agendas. The Starbrary group visualisations give us a taste of how it feels to work together in love and harmony.

It has been noticeable that the energy of the Starbrary crystals is strongly amplified when we connect with others. The more people who join a visualisation the stronger the energy that comes through. Online this sometimes crashes the live feed! I suspect it is all too much for our Earthly wi-fi to cope with.

Our Starbrary Custodians Facebook group is kept closed and is carefully moderated so that it is safe for members to be open about their experiences. To join us find the Starbrary Quartz Custodians group and send me a photo of yourself holding this book, or a photo of your Starbrary.

If you have a group of like-minded friends you could gather together to use the visualisations and exercises in the book. You might take turns in leading the visualisations for each other. You would also be welcome to attend one of my Messages from the Cosmos Experience Days.

A Starbrary Healing Circle

If you are part of an established healing circle you could introduce the Starbraries to raise the vibration of the healing the group sends. Ethically I believe we should never send healing to an individual unless they specifically request it. This is about respecting other people's boundaries.

When we send Starbrary healing in a circle we usually send to places where many people need healing. I add the caveat that the energy will be received by those who truly want it. In situations such as natural disasters or war zones there will be thousands of people who are desperate for help. Let the Starbrary healing find its way to those who will most welcome it.

Most of the visualisations in this book will work well in a group. Read through the instructions a couple of times before leading others through them. Do make sure that everyone has done their grounding and protection before you begin and take them through this process if necessary.

If you are sending healing within a circle you can agree a group focus for the healing so that the energy will be magnified by the group consciousness.

To strengthen the healing vibration within a circle you can create the Wheel of Light. The heart-based connections are made with pure beams of high vibrational Starbrary energy. They each flow towards the central Starbrary which then creates a unified beam of light for healing.

We have worked with the Wheel of Light effectively even when connecting with each other online and separated geographically.

The Wheel of Light

Each participant will hold a Starbrary quartz at their heart chakra. A larger Starbrary should be placed in the centre of the Circle, ideally supported so that it can stand upright.

Make the Cosmic Connection together (page 93).

Imagine you are standing in a circle holding your Starbraries. A beam of light flows clockwise around the outside of the circle making a continuous circuit protecting all the participants.

Visualise a huge Starbrary quartz point standing in the centre of the Circle, pointing upwards towards the Cosmos. You each focus on your heart centre and the Starbrary quartz you hold there. Light beams out from the Starbrary you hold towards the huge Starbrary in the centre. You see brilliant white beams of light connecting each individual to the central Starbrary. The light looks like spokes of a wheel connecting to the central hub. Now the energy of the group is unified.

The healing light you each channel flows into the central Starbrary. There it combines, forming a unified bright beam of light which is emitted from the tip of the crystal. The light shines out from the point of the Starbrary and flows to its intended destination.

When the healing is complete thank the central Starbrary, your individual Starbraries and any Star beings. Visualise the spokes of light fading away. Your individual Starbrary beams of light return to their stars.

Ground your energies, holding grounding stones if you need them. Write up your journals and share your experiences in the Circle.

The Stargate

The Stargate

Steve and I with the Stargate at the Crystal Enlightenment
Retreat in 2018. This was a Starbrary healing ritual we
designed for a large group experience.

Cathy, Monika and Carrie modelling their fabulous tin foil hats for a competition on the last night of the 2018 Retreat.

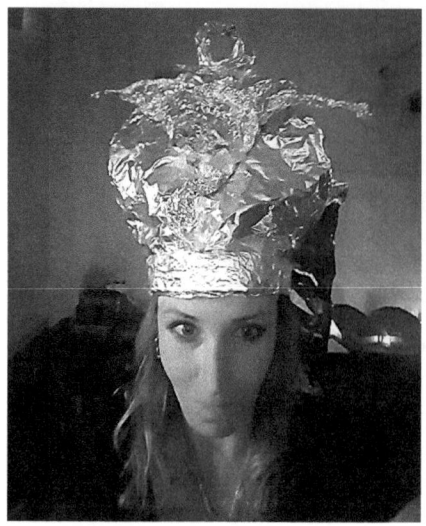

Our winner Louise with her extraordinary tin foil extravaganza.

Don't forget to enjoy yourself on your spiritual journey!

About the Author

Lauren D'Silva lives in Llandrindod Wells, a small Victorian spa town in the heart of Wales, with her husband, Shaman Steve Deeks-D'Silva.

Lauren has been exploring healing and spiritual development for over 20 years. She specialises in resolving past life issues and in relationship healing. She's had plenty of personal experience in these areas and shared her own story of spiritual awakening in her previous book 'Light behind the Angels'.

Lauren is Principal of Touchstones School of Crystal Therapy. She has completed six years as Chair of the Affiliation of Crystal Healing Organisations (ACHO). ACHO was established in the UK over 30 years ago to agree training standards for Crystal Healing. ACHO maintains a Register for qualified Practitioners who have trained with ACHO Member Schools.

At the time of writing Steve is Mayor of Llandrindod Wells and Lauren is the Mayor's Consort. Llandrindod was built upon its healing waters and the official emblem of the town portrays the healing Goddess Hygeia. Steve's Mayoral chain has a beautiful enamelled medallion of the Goddess which he is proud to wear over his heart.

Join the Touchstones newsletter list to receive regular updates. Why not come to a Masterclass, an Experience Day, or join one of Lauren and Steve's Retreats?

If you live too far away to receive healing or attend courses in person you may book one to one tuition via Skype, or distant healing, subject to Lauren's availability.

Stay in Touch with Touchstones

Join the Starbrary Quartz Custodians Facebook group. We keep this group a very safe and secure space to share. You'll be asked for a photo of your Starbraries or a 'selfie' with this book to be admitted.

Sign up to the Touchstones newsletter, or look at the diary page of Touchstones School of Crystal Therapy for details of upcoming courses and events:
www.crystal-therapy.co.uk

Book a healing with Lauren or arrange a guidance session via Skype
Email: lauren@touchstones-therapies.co.uk

Lauren's husband Steve Deeks-D'Silva has over 10 years of professional experience as a Shamanic exorcist. He has cleared thousands of people and homes all over the World. If you feel you may have an entity issue visit:
www.entity-removal.co.uk

Sourcing Starbraries

Starbrary quartz crystals are rare as they come from just one specific area of the Minas Gerais region of Brazil.

Lauren has a small stock of Starbraries for sale at the time of writing. Contact Lauren through Facebook, or email her:

lauren@touchstones-therapies.co.uk

Prices include postage to the UK. International buyers will be charged for trackable postage and will be liable for any additional taxes or import duties.

Picture credits

Cover designed using canva.com

All photos author's own apart from:

Page 8 Milky Way through Trees canva.com
Page 92 Ornamental Beautiful Card: An Vino/Bigstock.com
Page 111 St Nicholas of Bari banishing the Storm by Bicci di
Lorenzo: Photo is of author's print of this painting
Page 116 Used with Sherille's kind permission
Page 126 Hands holding Earth: Digital Storm/Bigstock.com
Page 133 Mysterious Entrance to New Life:
Egal/Bigstock.com
Page 156 Photos belong to Retreat participants, used here
with their kind permission
Page 157 Blue Spiral Galaxy with Starfield:
Pitris/Bigstock.com